CREATING the CARING CONGREGATION

CREATING THE CARING CONGREGATION

HAROLD H. WILKE

Foreword by Dr. Karl Menninger

Abingdon

Nashville

CREATING THE CARING CONGREGATION

Copyright © 1980 by Abingdon

Library of Congress Cataloging in Publication Data
WILKE, HAROLD.
  Creating the caring congregation.
  Bibliography: p.
  1 Church work with the handicapped. I. Title.
  BV4460.W48   261.8'324   79-28626

ISBN 0-687-09815-7

Scripture quotations unless otherwise noted are from the Revised
Standard Version of the Bible, copyrighted 1946, 1952, © 1971, 1973, by
the Division of Christian Education of the National Council of the
Churches of Christ in the U.S.A., and used by permission.

Scripture quotations noted Goodspeed are from The Complete Bible, an
American Translation, by J. M. Powis Smith and Edgar J. Goodspeed,
copyright 1939 by the University of Chicago Press. Used by permission.

Quotation from *The Cotton Patch Version of Paul's Epistles,* by Clarence
Jordan, published by Association Press, used by permission of Follett
Publishing Company.

MANUFACTURED BY THE PARTHENON PRESS AT
NASHVILLE, TENNESSEE, UNITED STATES OF AMERICA

ACKNOWLEDGMENTS

This volume is the result of an action-research project. Many people and groups were involved in its beginnings and its continuing history. Only a few can be named:

The Lilly Endowment, for the first major grant, providing support for the formal beginning.

The United Church of Christ, for significant financial support at the beginning, and for the time of the Director of the Council for Church and Ministry on occasional leaves, during the last five years of his service.

The New Samaritan Corporation, North Haven, Connecticut, which provided administrative support and liaison.

The Walter Scott Foundation, a primary supporter in the last two years.

Several voluntary health-oriented organizations, providing personnel and financial support, including the National Easter Seal Society and Goodwill Industries.

A host of local churches and other judicatories within the United Church of Christ, the United Presbyterian Church in the U.S.A., and the Roman Catholic Church.

Personnel who have served the Healing Community in its

action-research program in several cities include: Mr. Jack McClosky and the Reverend Dr. Norman E. Leach of San Francisco, Dr. John Harms of Indianapolis, Dr. O. Walter Wagner and Mrs. Jan Adkins of St. Louis, Mr. Charles Noell of New York. Dr. Ferdinand Schlingensiepen, Dr. Ernst Marquardt, and Dr. Kurt-Alphons Jochheim in Germany and Lady Hamilton and Mrs. Ann Henshall in England have been particularly helpful.

The members of the Board of Directors of Healing Community, particularly the Reverend Dr. Paul W. Yinger and the Reverend Dr. Roger Johnson, first two chairpersons, and Mr. Kenneth Preston, present chair, and other members of the Board of Directors and Advisory Board, have been constant in support and encouragement in the entire work of Healing Community, including the writing of this volume.

The Reverend Arthur E. Higgins has provided personal encouragement and administrative support through the New Samaritan Corporation.

Some of my words used here have appeared previously in a number of journals and books. For the use of some sentences or even paragraphs often unquoted, but previously published, thanks are due to *The Christian Century,* the *Archives of Physical Medicine and Rehabilitation,* the *Journal of Social Issues, The Christian Ministry, Journal of Theological Education,* and to the publishers of the following books: *Great the Man,* Harold H. Wilke (Philadelphia: Christian Education Press, 1945); *Strengthened with Might,* by Harold H. Wilke (Philadelphia: Westminster Press, 1952), *Partners in Life* (Geneva: W.C.C., 1979).

Joan Ballantyne has been patient and efficient in retyping the reedited versions of the manuscript.

And finally, for Peg, most helpful and long-suffering, enduring a husband's absences on trips plus the strewing about of papers, overflowing from the study into the dining room and living room.

Harold H. Wilke

Foreword

I first met Harold Wilke through an earlier book of his sent to me by Seward Hiltner. On the strength of that book, I invited him to lecture at the new veterans' hospital, designed as a teaching hospital for the Veterans' Administration and related to the Menninger Foundation School of Psychiatry. His first visit told me that however lucid and cogent his writing is, his presence makes it all sharper.

He arrived on a day when I was busy in my office, like everyone else, working with our new responsibilities for taking care of thousands of veterans. Through the door came this young man who introduced himself as Harold Wilke, the new chaplain. I rose to greet him.

"I can't shake hands with you," he said, "I never had hands." As he spoke, his face, smile, and friendly attitude conveyed more than any handshake could have done.

As he sat and talked, he brought forth a notebook from his side coat pocket and a pen for writing and acted in every way like a man who had no handicap. "This is true," he said. "I was expected by my parents to do everything my brothers did, and I learned alternative ways—toes instead of fingers."

I was developing a concept later called "Weller than Well," and somehow I saw this reflected in Harold Wilke. Perhaps the physical handicap that people see, in spite of his independence, has enabled him to understand people who have to make special efforts to keep up. I invited him to join our staff as a chaplain. Working with patients, his condition would be immediately recognized by them as affording an understanding of feelings they might not convey to the average visitor or doctor. Perhaps he could help all of us realize how a handicap can be overcome.

This he certainly did. Patients loved him, so did the nurses and doctors, including me. He inspired hope and renewed efforts in hundreds. He influenced me, too; he made me ashamed of lamenting apparent lacks, incapacities, and difficulties.

What a wonderful concept the Healing Community is. This book tells how every congregation can become one. Harold Wilke's whole life now is absorbed in the development of this idea, involving the religious community in a mainstreaming effort for all persons with various kinds of handicaps—physical, mental, emotional, and even spiritual.

Any community that Harold Wilke is in could be a healing community, but he has tried to shape the development of one that can be initiated and utilized by others whom it inspires.

Karl A. Menninger, M.D.

Contents

Preface

A special junction in history has come to pass. An emerging minority called "the handicapped" is now raising before our entire society, including the religious community, its own statement of identity and its sense of rightful appropriation of opportunity for achievement.

Our secular society is responding in positive and widespread ways, through legislation, regulations, voluntary agency action and publicity.

But what of the churches and synagogues? Some of us are running scared lest we fail at this critical juncture of expressed need on the part of handicapped persons.

Let us recapture our charter in the religious community. From the beginning our scriptures have affirmed the value of each individual in the sight of God, and this ages-old teaching must constantly be renewed.

Church and synagogues have been asking for help in

specific ways. Here are some answers to specific and general questions.

This book sets forth guidelines for the congregation attempting to respond to the needs of handicapped individuals.

The action-research program from which these guidelines emerged was formally begun on January 1, 1974, in four cities in the United States, along with some concomittant activity in England and Germany. They summarize the findings of those groups.

The Healing Community project actually had its beginning in the late sixties, arising out of deep concern about the policy of taking persons out of institutions and placing them in the community. With a keen appreciation of the potential voluntary help of nearly one hundred million members of churches, parishes, and synagogues, we present these guidelines with the deepest possible hope for their implementation in congregations all across the country.

CHAPTER ONE

Entertaining Angels Unawares

Do you remember months ago when you first saw that nondescript person in the congregation? His clothes were more than a little out of style, and he seemed so shy. Was it difficult for you to welcome him? And then, just recently, one of your close church friends told you how this man had come to his rescue in a sudden, critical situation and almost literally saved his life. Do you remember what your feelings were about the nondescript person then? How surprised you were. How foolish you felt for underrating him. How determined you were that the next time you would try to look a little more deeply into the life of this stranger or new church member.

We do this often, entertain angels unawares. We respond to people without realizing the inner beauty and strength they have. We only see the outer shell, the husk, and all too often we are guided merely by that.

The Scriptures have a classic story about it. Immediately after Jesus' death on the cross, two of his disciples were making their way to Emmaus. Jesus stepped in beside them, but their eyes were not attuned to recognize him. They simply talked with him as if he were a stranger.

When they arrived at their destination, they urged him to come in with them to eat and to rest before going on. Jesus did so, and as he blessed the bread at suppertime, suddenly their eyes were opened and they knew him for their Lord.

The two disciples had entertained this angel unawares. They even spoke of how their hearts had burned within them as they walked with Jesus. But they did not know him until they invited him in to sup with them and to rest.

Angels are constantly in our midst. They are persons like that new church member mentioned above; sometimes they are people to whom we pay negative rather than no attention at all. They are within your congregation, they are within the outer limits of the fellowship as well, and they are in your neighborhood.

This little book tells about one such group, persons we have in our midst, but usually a little farther away, who are called the handicapped. They are the physically disabled. They are the retarded. They are the persons with grave emotional problems. Many of them seem like the rest of us, but the physically disabled, of course, carry their difference in that outer hulk, the shell, the body. They walk with a crutch; they arrive in a wheelchair; they walk very slowly up the steps, pausing for breath at the third and the sixth; they use some prosthetic device like a steel hook.

We know that these people are different. But quite often we take the difference to be negative, and think that somehow they are totally different from us. Ironically, we do not remember that even the eyeglasses we wear are medically called prosthetic appliances, and false teeth as well. But when the prosthetic device is attached to the arm or leg of a person, somehow it seems to make him almost totally different.

To arrive at an awareness of the angels in our midst, we must build bridges and surmount barriers. Barriers of attitudes stand in the way of understanding and acceptance. They stand between person and person. On either side of the barrier, each person extends outward to many persons, to institutions, and even to countries. A ripple effect takes place; these attitudinal barriers, therefore, may be immensely more difficult to overcome than the architectural ones, difficult as those are.

This barrier of attitude begins inside the individual; it is in me. It is not something out there. It is not a thing, such as a building with steps. Since it is within myself, it may not even be based on fact in regard to the other person, but it clearly is a fact within myself.

How can I deal with this barrier? How much should it really concern me?

So my step is simply to move away. Even as I turn aside irresolutely, or sharply turn my back and go the other way, I feel nagging questions within me. These questions have to do with how much that barrier of attitude really reflects something within myself, and I have to ask whether I have dealt with this internal problem of my own. I have the haunting feeling that my accepting the reality of this attitudinal barrier actually has to do with my acceptance of myself; it involves questions of my own identity and my own place in space and time. Is failure to accept this barrier on the outside, so to speak, really a reflection of my failure to accept myself?

So the two are intertwined, accepting myself and accepting others. Who are the angels here? That angelic quality is mine too. And I can therefore go on to see the angels in others.

There is now a unique opportunity for the church as a whole to respond to persons with handicaps. Their number is legion. In a later chapter we will talk about who they are and something about how many. At this point we will consider our own experience, that they are here, and that we know both from some individual encounter in our lives and from a philosophical and religious view, that these persons are individuals of ultimate worth in the sight of God, even as we are.

With so many of them, more than a tenth of our population in the United States, we can assume that about a tenth of our congregation's membership would be these disabled and handicapped persons. And yet we know by our experience that very few of them are in the congregation. What is the reason? The answer leaps to us at once, and we realize that many of these persons feel so unwanted that they simply stay away from public gatherings, even from church. They are therefore the ones who are out of sight, so are out of mind. We do not think about them, because they are not around us or within our immediate fellowship.

It is evident that society itself, with its attitudes and its architecture, is the basic handicapping condition.

The time is ripe now for the church to take the lead in helping the whole community facilitate the coming together, the integration, of all persons within the body of the community. And we start with the church. Better yet, we start individually with ourselves. We start with me.

To begin with myself I must recognize in all honesty that these hesitations are present. "I *will* do this," really starts with, "I must first see all the underbrush in the way before I can take this step." Make no mistake about it, this underbrush is present, these impediments in my own emotional responses are very real. I must be able to recognize the fact of their existence and learn how to deal with them.

My first fear is that somehow this disability of the other individual is catching. It might actually infect me. As soon as I say this in words, I recognize how foolish the concept is, but the fear, usually unconscious to me, is actually present.

A second fear is related to the first; this unknown thing out there attached to this person is threatening to me in still other ways. I do not understand how the threat exists; I only know that I am afraid. The person with the obvious physical handicap represents the unknown, and I am scared of the unknown.

For a long time I thought my wife was deathly afraid of snakes, because once when I called to her, "Step to one side; a snake is near the path," she became extremely agitated, crying out, "I can't see it!" Finally when she did see it, she was able to deal with the problem. It is not seeing the thing—not understanding the problem, not seeing the specific components of something before us that has to be dealt with—this is the frightening part for us.

The third fear is more agonizing, because it represents something that is actually in me; it symbolizes my own weakness and my own inability. It makes me cry out in recognition of my own handicaps and my own shortcomings. In this case, the fear is not something created by that thing out there, it is what that thing actually induces within me, so that I am now torn within myself.

Dreams of Superman being within me have long since disappeared. I have long since understood that I am pretty much like other people. While I may not be exactly a klutz, there are still many things in the world that I cannot do. I cannot become president of the United States or of U.S. Steel. I cannot make my body over the way the ads say the body should be. Worse than that, this vulnerability seems to describe not only my present situation but also the future. It won't get better, and I do know that some day I am going to die.

When I see someone who is severely crippled, my fears respond to this inner anxiety about the vulnerability, the shortcomings and handicaps existing within myself.

A friend with an amputated hand expressed to his religious superior his desire to enter the ministry. The minister responded, "You can't possibly do the jobs that the ministry requires, and I will not recommend you for this." Looking back on that sharp "you can't" from his position as a very successful minister, my friend said it took him years to understand that an unconscious process was involved. The religious leader, quite inept and bungling in his job, unconsciously was saying, "Since I find it difficult to do a ministry with both hands, how can this chap do it with ony one?"

ACCEPTANCE OF SELF

I begin this internal search—this look at myself—recognizing I must accept what I see there. I begin not with an oughtness, namely, that I ought to feel different about these fears, or that I ought to respond more positively toward the person with the handicap who has induced these fears within me or called them to the surface in me. It is instead my recognition that these fears do exist. I have to start with what is there, rather than with what ought to be present or ought not to be present.

CHAPTER TWO

The Faith

Wholeness, becoming one within oneself, having one purpose, is a constant aim for the Christian. The Christian philosopher Kierkegaard called it "to will one thing." We do not want to be at war within ourselves, in tension within our own mind and spirit.

The search for salvation, of course, takes many forms. The flood of books on the market on overcoming anxiety, finding healing, becoming a whole person—all attest to the human striving for some kind of unity within the psyche, within the person.

Just as there are may forms of anxiety, so are there many forms of response. A dozen new schools of psychological response, ranging from est to Primal Scream to many others, have been established to heal the individual. The Christian faith has produced its forms of healing response, from radio and television healers, self-styled, to Christian philosophers who propose various kinds of answers, often a mixture of the secular and Christian.

Paradoxically, the Christian faith provides one of the strongest negative responses to acceptance of persons with handicaps; while at the same time it promises, and indeed fulfills in its faith, the overcoming of handicapping conditions.

The first response is rooted in a biblical position which states explicitly that persons with physical disabilities may not be leaders in the church, although they may receive from the church. This position then suggests that the only form of response to this handicapping condition is for actual healing to take place.

The second response is found in the faith expressed both in the parables and healing of Jesus and in the Letters of Paul. It is the *imputation* of wholeness and salvation, corresponding to the imputation of righteousness, which has long been a bedrock theme of biblical theology, lifted to high visibility by Reformation theology. The imputation of righteousness holds that the human being cannot *earn* salvation. Luther's restatement of this basic biblical theme was the triumphant conclusion of his anguished search for salvation. He felt again and again the weight of Paul's writing: I do not do the good I want, but the evil I do not want is what I do (Rom. 7:19). His avid reading in the Letter to the Romans and in other letters led him to restate that central New Testament concept, that man does not live by his own deeds, that the human does not earn his salvation, that God in love for all humankind graciously grants—imputes—the righteousness that cannot be earned, the righteousness in Christ, to the rest of humankind.

In the light of this expression of the search for salvation in New Testament writings we see another form of that gift of salvation to humanity, namely that of wholeness.

The doctrine of the imputation of wholeness, the free

and gracious granting of wholeness, has had difficult going in modern times. Part of the difficulty lies in various forms of perversion of the Christian faith, perhaps the most egregious being the one that states the person's own responsibility in strength of faith, or lack of it, having to do with his blindness or her impairment. Almost all of us have heard or seen expressions of this particular perversion. A blind person notes, "This perfect stranger comes up to me and says, 'If only your faith were strong enough, you could see!' " We cringe at this, but persons with obvious physical impairments, most particularly blindness, get this kind of response sometimes daily. A hostile statement to a total stranger, it is even worse a perversion of the Christian faith. The doctrine of "the imputation of wholeness," the heart of the gospel, is that God loves us unreservedly, and in Christ has given the divine being for our own sins and shortcomings. The salvation we cannot earn for ourselves, the wholeness we cannot achieve individually, God offers to us in the gracious gift of Christ on the cross of Calvary. We therefore see our handicaps and the handicaps of others through the lenses of God, namely that the handicaps have been overcome; they no longer exist in God's ultimate perspective. If the Lord has removed this blemish, who are we to say of ourselves or of others that the blemish exists?

As these words are read, the perceptive reader, whole and able-bodied, recognizes immediately that we are not talking about some people "out there." We are talking about ourselves. We are talking about each Christian who has gone through the fires of self-doubt and anxiety, who has walked the way of emotional illness, who has trembled in despair over his personal life, or her family situation. We are all in this boat together. Everyone of us has now or has had at some point, or will have, a disabling condition, an illness, physical or emotional, a dropping of intellectual levels, a time of lost achievement. This message of the gospel speaks to everyone of us.

"Jesus loves me, this I know, for the Bible tells me so." We sang these words in Sunday school, perhaps, but they are not an unsophisticated expression of our faith. The great theologian Karl Barth calls these two verses the very heart of the Christian faith: In Christ God was reconciling the world to himself (II Cor. 5:19); "For God so loved the world. . . . (John 3:16). These two verses state that God was indeed in Christ, overcoming all that was considered evil and negative in humankind.

But there is more. Within the biblical tradition itself, not just interpretation, there is a tremendous negative response to physical disability, and we need to see this quite clearly. In the very center of the book of Leviticus, "the giving of the law," God says that no one who has any kind of impairment may serve at the Lord's table. While such a person may eat of the food, he is not permitted to serve it.

Let us look at the ways in which the conditions of blemish are seen in the biblical tradition.

In the Law and the Prophets, from Genesis through Zechariah, numbers of handicapping conditions are mentioned. The Hebrew term for blemish seems to have originally meant a black spot. The word "denotes anything abnormal or deviating from a given standard, whether physical, moral, or ritualistic." Numbers of references point out that the law requires animals offered for sacrifice to be without blemish. The Levitical statements say it without equivocation:

None of your descendants, from generation to generation, who has a defect, may draw near to offer his God's food; for no one who has a defect may come near, no one who is blind, or lame, or has any perforations, or has a limb too long, no one who has a fractured foot, or a fractured hand, or is a hunchback, or has a cataract, or a defect of eyesight, or scurvy, or scabs, or crushed testicles—no one of the descendants of Aaron, the priest, who has a defect, may come near to offer the Lord's sacrifices; since he has a defect, he may not come near to offer his God's food. He may eat his God's food, some of the most sacred as well as the sacred; only he must not approach the veil, nor come near the altar, because he has a defect in him, lest he profane my sanctuaries; for it is I, the Lord, who consecrate them. [Lev. 21:17-23 Goodspeed and Smith]

A special set of statutes governed the priestly blessing, which was separate from the being a priest. Maimonides lists six such disqualifying blemishes: defective articulation of speech; malfunction of face, hands, or feet, or unusual appearance of hands, as discolored; moral delinquency, as idolatry or murder; immature, beard not fully grown; drunken; unclean, not having washed the hands. Also listed is the son of an unlawful marriage because such is not a priest at all.

Perfection of the body was a symbol of the perfection of the soul, according to Philo. For Maimonides, it was to underscore the honor and respect due the temple, since the multitude "does not appreciate a man for his true worth, but for the perfection of his limbs and the beauty of his garments."

It is quite clear that as far as physical blemishes were concerned, "The test was purely pragmatic; thus if the cohen was so well known that his blemish raised no curiosity, the ban was removed. Although the prohibition against a blemished priest officiating in the temple is given in the Bible, the Talmud justifies it by interpreting the word *shalom* in Numbers 25:12 as *shalem* (whole)."[1]

Let us not judge Leviticus too harshly. Remember that the statements in the law and in the historical books against persons with handicaps are also the teachings of the other cultures of that time. The purpose is simple and good: the best is to be given to the Lord. The priests of the Lord were to be selected from the finest specimens of men. Furthermore, when physical perfection did not exist, but when even the physical impairment did not disturb the congregation, it was at that point of no consequence.

The idea of the Suffering Servant stresses that the one who comes ultimately to give life and hope to humankind is the one who suffers for humankind, who gives himself for that humanity. The Suffering Servant exemplifies God's ultimate concern for humankind, giving the assurance that underneath all of us are the everlasting arms. The Suffering Servant is also one who responds to the needs of all persons. In a Western society that has so often rejected the handicapped, at least at the unconscious level, and has made such persons the *object* of mission and oftentimes of pity and scorn, the Suffering Servant shows God's concern not only for the able and privileged persons of this world but also for the apparently forsaken.

Still other deeply positive feelings about the handicapped are seen in Judaism. There is a Talmud citation:

Only one single man was created in the world, to teach that, if any man has caused a single soul to perish, scripture imputes it to him as though he had caused a whole world to perish, and if any man saves a life, scripture imputes it to him as though he had saved the whole world. Again, but a single man was created for the sake of peace among mankind that none should say to his fellow, my father was greater than your father, also, that the heretics should not say that there are many ruling powers in heaven. Again but a single man was created to proclaim the greatness of God, for man stamps many coins with one die and they are all like to one another, but God has stamped every man with a die of the first man, yet not one of them is like his fellow. Therefore, everyone must say, for my sake the world was created!

Judaism holds that such theological dignity then is conferred on every person. Beyond this, the rabbis attributed to humanity, although in their sense this is each individual, a task and a status that could not be predicated of any other created thing on earth. Two famed rabbis speak to this. Rabbi Abba Bar Yudan states: "All that God has declared to be unclean in animals, he has pronounced desirable in man. In animals he has declared, blind or broken or maimed or having a wen" (Lev. 22:22) to be unserviceable, but in men he has declared the crushed and broken heart to be desirable. The other, Rabbi Alexander, said: "If a private person uses broken vessels, it is a disgrace to him, but God uses broken vessels, as it is said, the Lord is nigh to the broken-hearted" (Ps. 36:18). A myriad of similar quotations may be found throughout Jeremiah, Isaiah, and the Psalms.

Other religions express the same point.

For the Christian the norm is Jesus' own response. What does the New Testament say about handicapping conditions? How did our doctrine of the imputation of wholeness come about within the New Testament? Let us look carefully at Jesus' own words and actions and the statements of other New Testament books.

JESUS' WORD: IT'S IRRELEVANT

The critically important reference to any kind of handicap in the New Testament is the Johannine story of the man blind from his birth (John 9:1-7). In the Goodspeed and Smith translation, it reads:

As he passed along, he saw a man who had been blind from his birth. His disciples asked him,

"Master, for whose sin was this man born blind? For his own, or for that of his parents?"

Jesus answered,

"It was neither for his own sin nor for that of his parents, but to let what God can do be illustrated in his case. We must carry on the work of him who has sent me while the daylight lasts. Night is coming, when no one can do any work. As long as I am in the world, I am a light for the world."

As he said this he spat on the ground and made clay with the saliva, and he put the clay on the man's eyes, and said to him,

"Go and wash them in the Pool of Siloam"—a name which means One who has been sent. So he went and washed them, and went home able to see.

The following verses indicated the wrangling which went on between him, his parents, and the neighbors, as to what happened, with strong questioning by the Pharisees and the blind man's response, "He put some clay on my eyes, and I washed them, and I can see" (v. 15b).

Later, the Pharisees excluded the blind man from the synagogue. Their charge was, "You were born in utter sin, and are you trying to teach us?" Jesus learned of this and sought him out; after the blind man fell on his knees before him, Jesus said, "I have come into the world to judge men, that those who cannot see may see, and that those who can see may become blind." Some of the Pharisees who heard this asked, "Are we blind too?" Jesus answered, "If you were blind, you would be guilty of no sin, but as it is, you say 'We can see'; so your sin continues" (v. 41).

Throughout the New Testament, Jesus' response to disability and other handicapping conditions is any of these: to heal that condition, to consider it irrelevant, and to seek justice, as in the attempt to change the ritual law on healing.

Let us look at each one of these responses of Jesus in the Johannine story.

The first is the flat denial that sin has anything to do with this handicapping condition. "Neither sinned," Jesus answered, referring to both the parents and to the man himself. It is the most definitive statement we have in the New Testament that sin is not the causative factor in a physically handicapping condition. (There are other statements by Jesus in other situations that imply the relationship of illness and sin, or estrangement from God, and we must consider them later.) This story, the man born blind, carries Jesus' unequivocal and definitive statement that sin did not cause the congenital blindness.

The second response of our Lord is that the blindness is a mark of the Kingdom; it is a sign that God uses persons in specific ways to fulfill the divine intention for the world. In the Goodspeed and Smith translation used here, the phrase is "to let what God can do be illustrated in his case." Jesus dealt with the underlying fact of the situation, namely that the man was blind and that this blindness was not caused by sin. The fact that the man had continued to live in faith (he was a member of the synagogue) that something could be done about himself is the basis for Jesus' phrase, "What God can do . . . in his case." Granted the *fact* of the illness or in this case the blindness, it is how the person deals with the negative condition that reflects the God-given character of the individual. What God can do in this case where a person, born blind, continues to have faith, illustrates precisely God's intent for every person. How we cope with a situation, how we respond to the low spots and the high spots of our lives, how we seize the opportunity of picking up the rusty blade when the burnished sword is not available to us determines the kind of help God can give us. What God can do is illustrated in the continuing faith of this individual.

A third meaning in this story is of critical importance, and is seen in the fact that there is no hiatus whatever between Jesus' statement that God's strength is illustrated in this man's case and the following phrase, "We must carry on the work of him who has sent me while the daylight lasts." The *we* includes the blind man even before he was healed. We, all of us, must do the work of God.

There is a second parable that defines the place of the handicapped in the life of the Kingdom. It is in the middle of the fourteenth chapter of Luke. We remember the story of a householder who proposed a huge banquet to which he invited his special friends, the affluent and well-to-do. You remember the excuses they gave: "I have bought five yoke of oxen, and I go to examine them" ["I just bought a new sports car, and I've got to try it out"]; "I have married a wife, and therefore I cannot come." The householder, angered, asks his friends to go out into the highways and byways, to bring in the poor and the maimed. Jesus then states, "For every one who exalts himself will be humbled, and he who humbles himself will be exalted" (v. 11). He goes on to say: "Do not invite your friends or your brothers or your kinsmen or rich neighbors, lest they also invite you in return, and you be repaid. But when you give a feast, invite the poor, the maimed, the lame, the blind, and you will be blessed, because they cannot repay you. You will be paid at the resurrection of the just" (vv. 12-14).

The kingdom of God is not complete without the poor and the maimed! And each member thereof is not complete, or has hope of salvation, unless his own lameness or her own blindness, the negative aspects of their lives, are included.

For the Christian community the one lost sheep is the one for whom the Shepherd leaves all the others to save. In Jesus' picture of the Day of Judgment, he expresses the idea that God in Christ comes to the person who visits the sick, the prisoners, and those in need. The nail-pierced hands of Jesus, the stigmata, are the hands of one who cares for the stigmatized, who are in manifold ways pierced by the turned aside eyes of fellow human beings. In word and action Jesus sets the handicapped directly within the circle of unity of the Christian church.

New Testament theology also builds heavily on the Pauline argument that the individual is made perfect in weakness, that God has chosen the weak of the world to demonstrate life's meanings to the wise and the strong. It is not weakness itself that is to be glorified, but the fact that in weakness one can see clearly God's intent for the world, that is, for the power of Christ to dwell within one.

The doctrine of grace holds that we are accepted into the love, not by our deeds or by our being, but by the grace of God. Thus a person's power, beauty, majesty, and strength all combined cannot save him; salvation comes through grace. Illness, physical handicap, decrepitude, old age, or mental retardation cannot destroy a person in the sight of God; he or she is saved by grace. The condition of everyone of us before God is the same.

There is also the utilitarian question. Why debate theological meanings when these persons are here? We acknowledge their presence among us and indeed see them in us. Without searching for reasons, without attempting to find the cause of evil and illness and pain in the world, we rather ask, What can we do? Jesus' answer at this point is found in his statement to the persons who asked him, "Who sinned, this man or his parents, that he was born blind?" Jesus' response was that neither sinned; then he went on to the next step: within the condition this person has, it is yet his duty and indeed his glorious privilege to praise God.

The messianic feast of Jesus and the "strength in weakness" statements of Paul are cornerstones for the doctrine that within the very nature of the church itself weakness is present, so that God may be glorified.

CHAPTER THREE

The Church Says No!

Even as there are ways beyond counting in which the church through its institutional life and its faith has helped individuals survive the terrors of loneliness and alienation, so also the church fails to fulfill such needs.

EXCLUSIVITY OF THE CHURCH

Mirroring the secular world, resistance to the presence of handicapped persons is a continuing blot upon the church's attempt at openness and inclusivity.

Socially alienated persons are too often rejected by the local congregation and responded to, if at all, primarily in terms of a "mission" on the part of the church to these groups. These are the persons who are wounded or ill on the road to Jericho wherever we travel. On this road the church is often not the Good Samaritan, but the priest and the Levite passing by on the other side.

Perhaps it is the weight of the "no crippled clergy" in Leviticus that reaches across the years. For in the church today, Orthodox and Catholic, there are clear statements of doctrine opposing ministry by persons with physical disabilities, and what is *de jure* in these two churches is *de facto* in Protestantism.

Orthodox churches go back to very early statements: The Council of Trullo (AD 692) confirms Orthodox canons dating from the middle of the fourth century, with Canon 77 stating: "If anyone be deprived of an eye, or leg, but in other respects be worthy of a bishopric, he may be ordained, for the defect of the body does not defile a man, but the pollution of the soul," and in Canon 78: "But if a man be deaf or blind, he may not be made a bishop, not indeed as if he were thus defiled, but that the affairs of the church may not be hindered."

Justification for the presence of a handicap barring an individual from serving as a priest is presented in this modern statement:

The importance of these canonical restrictions may be difficult to fathom for those who are not from a liturgical oriented tradition. However, an Orthodox priest is foremost a minister of the cult; his primary responsibility is to lead the faithful in liturgical prayer, and although individual pastoral duties and the development of his own ritual life are also incumbent upon him, they devolve from his role as leader of sacramental worship. Any personal disability which interferes with that liturgical function makes it impossible for a man to be ordained a priest for to ordain a handicapped man who would, for example, be able only to teach or only to counsel would be a dismemberment of the priestly vocation (Stephen Plumlee, *Partners in Life*. [Geneva: World Council of Churches, 1979], p. 114.)

The Catholic canon law doctrine expressing this understanding is called *Admiratio Populi,* the discomfort or distraction within members of the congregation caused by that public figure whose outward appearance would distract the congregation.

For the priestly life, the primary concerns center around a doctrine or role widely accepted within Protestant as well as Catholic circles, that the priest is "a man for others," the "one for others." This role—"before the congregation," "in front of the congregation," "upfront"—is very public in administering the sacraments, preaching the Word, and serving other human beings within and without the congregation. This public nature of priestly expression, for the Catholic Church of recent years as well as for the Levitical priest three thousand years ago, recognized the admixture of the various elements of response within a public to the person acting for them.

PRACTICE IN PROTESTANTISM

The practice of Protestantism, while not canonical, is pervasively negative.

That unwritten Protestant doctrine has historically deterred physically disabled persons from entering the ministry, since it is of course admitted that some forms of disability or disfigurement could cause discomfort or distraction within the congregation. The writer is convinced that one of the unspoken reasons for reluctance to admit women into the clergy has been this conscious sense of the male leadership that the woman is "incomplete," that her very femaleness would cause this distraction or discomfort (and probably the writer's reaction to this was his primary reason for ordaining one of the first women into the ministry of his denomination).

A blind Protestant minister recently urged the creation of a listing of Protestant ministers with disabilities. Already a hundred names are on the list, without any research at all. Disabilities range from blindness to amputations to residual polio to spinal cord injury from accidents. With many of these the disability occurred after ordination. The church continues to raise serious questions about a disabled individual seeking to enter the ministry. Serious concern should be a requisite, of course, for one must be physically, mentally, and emotionally capable of fulfilling essential clergy requirements. But for the ecclesiastical committee to decline the proffer of service simply on the basis of a disability is wrong.

Among the Jewish faith groups, two professors in the Jewish Theological Seminary of New York, where there is a blind rabbinical student, assured me that there was no impediment whatever to accepting handicapped young men into the rabbinate because "they are really the teachers for the congregation."

CHURCH MEMBERS MIRROR THE SECULAR

But church people do not need to take their lead from the ordained; they can also mirror the negative attitudes of secular society. A recent study of attitudes toward handicapped as displayed in "the funnies" showed a marked division between very negative, with a relatively few very positive at the other end, and with none in between.

The device of not recognizing, simply not seeing the

person or the situation, is perhaps illustrated particularly in a survey at the University of Kansas some years ago. Under the leadership of Disabled in Action, a group of students, most of them using wheelchairs, persuaded the university to prepare curb-cuts throughout the university area so they could move their wheelchairs about freely on the campus. Six months later a questionnaire was distributed to representative groups on the campus. One would be both amazed and chagrined at the results. Ninety-five percent of the students said the curb-cuts were made so they could get their bicycles from street to sidewalk more easily; all the campus vendors said it was to make it easier for them to bring in supplies to service the buildings; young mothers with baby carriages thought it was for them. Most groups felt the device aided them, and they simply did not notice the one group of students who had instigated the architectural change. (Obviously the study indicates additionally that curb-cuts and other accessible changes in architecture benefit not only a relatively few but also a vast number of people.)

A study at the University of Kentucky asked for the ranking of acceptable disabilities. It showed that not severity but visibility of the disability affected the ranking most, with the most visible ones among the least tolerable.

At Dartmouth an eleven-year-study by Robert Kleck on attitudes toward disability found a double standard. The words, from "nondisabled" to "disabled", were positive and nice, but the physiological reactions—eye movement, sweat, heart rate and so on—showed anxiety, avoidance, and rejection. The double standard of course comes from the inappropriateness within society of outright rejection, so the nod and smile mask genuine interaction.

The prevalence of negative attitudes in the religious

community is noted by Dr. Frank Bowe in *Handicapping America*. He recognizes, though, that the example set by Jesus of seeking out and helping disabled people inaugurated a new period of sympathy toward persons with disabilities. Church men and women began to organize services for disabled persons, doing much that was needed, at which point Dr. Bowe sees all the rest of Christian service as suffused with a negative "provider-receiver relationship," which he charges continues to this day "to characterize charitable causes." Dr. Bowe adds, "Religious groups assumed a position as providers, a position of superiority and control."[1] The price was a stiff one for the receiver—dislocation, often, and subservience to the provider that carried with it a loss of autonomy.

The sharpest charge is "underlying the new charity was a conviction that Christian theology justified these actions on the grounds that disability was an indication of impurity and evidence of a soul that needed to be saved." This is widely accepted within the religious population. Even though the theological base of the faith denies such response, it is widely held, and sets the battle lines for us in the churches today.

The pervasiveness of the attitude is set forth by Gloria Maxson in the "Speaking Out" column in the September 21, 1977, issue of *Christian Century*. "As one of America's 30 million disabled or 'sickened-class' citizens—I find the attitudes are subtle and entrenched, and will change slowly," she says. As a chairbound polio-arthritis victim, she has encountered these attitudes:

(1) Outright rejection: The disabled are seated in the back; we are objects of pained and evasive glances; we are victimized by the assumption that we are inept and unable to "do" anything on a committee. In short, the word

"INvalid" is mispronounced "inVALid." We need to be known as valids. When a church member purrs, "I didn't call you, dear, because I wasn't sure you'd feel up to the job," perhaps she is being "kind," but I snarl in my best Mae West voice: "Well, call me up sometime and ask me, baby—give me the fun of saying No!" We need to develop what Alex Comfort advises for the aged: "Bloody-mindedness"—the spunk to raise hell in order to reveal heaven.

(2) Overacceptance: When we enter some churches, avid members swarm over us like a plague of locusts, proud of having a resident wreck or token kook to show off their vast liberalism. They betray the "brave little soldier" type of patronage in assuming that we are all unnaturally heroic, with special dispensation for bearing our crosses. We cannot cry out in pain and despair, for we are their "inspiration"—another alienating concept.

(3) Sanctimoniousness and pious tirades: We have all writhed under the hideous exhortations of the judgmental, who insist that "You don't need that surgery; you need the Savior." Or, "If you had real faith, you'd rise right up out of that chair." To such I send a reference to Matthew 4:5-7, where Satan tempts Jesus to cast himself down on the rocks, claiming God will preserve him, and Jesus refuses to put God to a foolish test. Harsh attitudes add to the burden of the handicapped and make a wheelchair a badge of shame, implying that we lack the courage to rehabilitate ourselves.

(4) Lack of outreach: My church preference is non-denominational, but of all the churches I called for grassroots grace and home help, Jehovah's Witnesses were the only ones to respond. I believe that all churches should offer this same grassroots grace to the handicapped: the

one-to-one caring of the truly Christlike community. The Witnesses are doing a basic and important work in society, though they are a much-maligned and misunderstood group.

A paraplegic friend of mine maintains, rather sadly: "Well, when space visitors finally arrive, we handicapped had better be sent out to welcome them. We won't be horrified by physical difference, having had to accept it in ourselves, so we won't see them as 'monsters' but as his 'other sheep, not of this pasture.' "

The no symbolized in inaccessible architecture must again be mentioned. Architectural openness is necessary in every area of society, including those areas where the person lives out social, personal, and cultural concerns.

Ironically, the concern for architecture dates back years, and yet so little has been done. It was a quarter century ago that this author published *Strengthened with Might* (Philadelphia: Westminster, 1955) in which he noted:

A new trend in church architecture is opening up more opportunities for the physically handicapped to participate in church activities. Some new churches are built in such a way that the person confined to a wheelchair may enter the church without difficulty and find a place in the sanctuary especially reserved for him. At several hospitals where I have served as chaplain there was room in the very front of the sanctuary and at the back of it for the wheelchair patients. Most important, there were no forbidding steps at the entrance to the chapel, steps that the wheelchair patients obviously cannot negotiate. Yet look at our traditionally built churches: ten steps—count them—up which one must climb in order to enter to worship. Worse, many of these are outside steps, wet, and slippery and dangerous; each step saying, 'no,' to the member in the wheelchair, the aged, the infirm, the ones with heart conditions, those with poor eyesight.

Few persons can forget the sight of a church high on a hill, imposing, majestic, part of which image comes from the hundred and ten concrete steps the worshiper climbs to enter its doors. One joke in the area is that the priest exacts penance not by asking for 210 Hail Marys, but simply by climbing the 210 steps to church.

The American Lutheran Church at its national level exacts a financial penalty from local churches that do not design their buildings to avoid barriers to the physically impaired. The Board of Service and Mission in America agreed that implications for loans from the church extension fund would ordinarily be refused if the plans do not conform to their barrier-free guidelines, titled *Space and the Physically Impaired*. Since church extension fund loans carry lower interest rates than commercial loans, local churches are encouraged financially, as well as morally, to build barrier-free buildings. The director of the division estimates that "it would cost 1 percent additional to insure barrier-free buildings," but the Reverend William J. Hanson admits that renovation of existing buildings is both expensive and difficult.

Interestingly, over six hundred ALC congregations had plans to make their buildings more accessible, an additional one thousand would like further information, but well over two thousand have no plans to alter existing structures. This Minneapolis-based denomination has a strong advocate in its division on ministry in the Reverend James Siefkes, a member of the Advisory Board of Healing Community.

Informed churches all across the country are beginning to ask themselves, "How can we cease saying no and turn to saying yes? How can we affirm not only the handicapped in our midst, but our church wholeness as well?

CHAPTER FOUR

The Church Says Yes!

The institutional church, being pushed and pulled by the emerging presence of the handicapped in the community, the compelling challenge to the religious community by individuals and groups in the disabled community, and a deeper theological awareness is now moving (still glacially) toward a new sense of acceptance of the handicapped in the mainstream of both church and community life.

Whether in mission to or mission with, the church has responded with the power of the accepting congregations.

An approach that has great potential for consciousness-raising within ordinary congregations is fulfilled by a group in Chicago. This group convenes its handicapped members once a month at a different church in the Chicago area. By prearrangement and invitation some twenty-five to one hundred physically disabled persons in wheelchairs converge upon a specific church, become a part of the worshiping congregation in the morning, have lunch, hosted by the church, and enjoy a time of fellowship in the afternoon.

The group of disabled individuals goes to various churches, but they do have favorites. "I hear they like to keep coming back to my church," said the minister of one large and prestigious church in a Chicago suburb, "because they know the senior minister is blind, one associate minister is female, and the other associate is a hippie."

Regular meetings are held on the first Sunday of each month, with a different church holding each meeting. The structure is simple. All participants are considered members, and management is under the responsibility of the board of directors, elected for one-year terms at the annual meeting. The board members elect their own officers; funds come from offerings taken each month.

Duplication of this program would seem to be relatively easy. It is described by Eleanor Roberts in the March 1979 issue of *The Christian Ministry:*

> To start, one or two people dedicated to the concept and who have the support of at least one church are required. Then the support of other churches must be enlisted. After adequate support is gained, contact with the handicapped can begin using health agencies as initial suppliers of names. Once a group is established, the project will grow by itself. [P. 15]

The pattern for the Saturday meeting begins early for volunteer drivers who pick up the participants at their homes and arrive at the church by midmoring. Plenty of time is allowed for the often-difficult process of getting from automobile to building. There are Bible groups, a hot lunch provided and served by the host church, fellowship, entertainment, and then finally an hour-long worship service in the sanctuary, with care for full participation by everyone.

What it means to the participant is immediately obvious. What it means to the church members may be seen partly in the activities, more deeply in the resultant feelings and attitudes. In at least one instance the activities involved: three choirs to provide musical entertainment and inspiration; three chapters of the women's society to provide and serve a noon meal and coffee and doughnuts to the drivers; twenty-six drivers to transport participants; sixteen strong men and boys to carry wheelchairs up and down the long flight of stairs; a group of young women from the high school fellowship to serve as hostesses, registrants, and guides. The diaconate served Communion; the minister conducted the service of worship. These and more added up to two hundred gifts by individuals, most given willingly. Volunteers are not always easy to find. Some people feel inadequate; Others have the apprehension arising from the fear of the unknown. Thus "proper preparation of the church members as to what project renewal is, who the participants are, and what the needs are is essential to the success" (Project Renewal, *The Christian Ministry* March 1979, p. 17).

Many special groups have come into existence to meet special needs for worship and fellowship. One that has been in existence now for twenty years in the Duluth, Minnesota, area is titled Hear-Us, acronym for Handicapped Ecumenical Annual Retreats Uniting Souls. A close Christ-centered weekend at a nearby Christian camp is planned by a committee made up of both disabled and able-bodied persons with the desire of furthering Christian ministry and fellowship or support from other Christians; it's not rare to hear one of the disabled retreatants say that he or she lives for Christ alone, that without God life would lose its meaning.

The program also sponsors a fall movie and a spring banquet, functions reaching perhaps one hundred adults and finding a new closeness to God for its members. See the section on resources, page 104.

Another one of these groups is the Southern Maine Association for Handicapped Persons, meeting monthly at the Woodfords Congregational Church in Portland, a church with a ramp that was built from the beginning. The church has augmented this with handicapped parking signs on the street, installed a new ramp marking doors with a handicapped decal, and created an accessible bathroom.

Some congregations composed entirely of persons with handicaps have been created. These separatist groups minister only to disabled persons. One example, with several subsidiaries in different parts of the country, is the Church of the Exceptional, in Macon, Georgia. This church has more than two hundred members, all with varying handicaps. Church architecture, worship, and congregational expectancy are geared to these persons with special needs. The stated philosophy is ultimately to integrate with "normal" congregations, but in the meantime, feeling unaccepted, these persons have opportunity to worship in the comfortable presence of individuals like themselves. Another group is Victim Missionaries, seven thousand strong, with chapters in a dozen states but based in the convent of Our Lady of the Snows in Belleville, Illinois, under the charismatic leadership of Father John Maronic. Not limited to Catholics, the group actually penetrates through its members many Catholic churches.

Still another expression of an approach separate from the

local congregation, yet combining both able-bodied and disabled, is used by the group Handicapped Enounter Christ. An entire three-day weekend is set at a retreat house, with about forty to fifty persons in attendance, one-half disabled and one-half able-bodied, totally directed toward the religious encounter. The religious retreat experience is not officially sanctioned within the organized church, but it is principally Roman Catholic in worship expression. Started in 1974, retreats have been held in the New York area almost monthly since 1976, and have extended to Boston, Philadelphia, Arizona, and a number of other places.

We still live in tension between the separatist way, creating a congregation specifically for retarded or handicapped, and the wholistic way of getting such persons involved in the local church. Even with the mainstream as the goal, it is sometimes architectural reasons alone that make a separate service of Christian worship necessary.

SPECIALIZED MINISTRIES WITHIN CHURCHES

Continuing specialized ministries under church auspices have been maintained for many years by the Episcopal Church, a number of Lutheran bodies, and many other denominations in greater or lesser degree. Such ministries stem sometimes from the national denominational offices; more often they have come out of diocesan or synodical responses, which then have spread to other areas of the church. The usual target groups for such ministries have been persons representing very specific difficulties, such as the deaf or the blind. Within a local area, members of churches will tacitly accept an ecumenical answer by simply pointing out that signing for the deaf is carried on at one or more specific churches in the city, and deaf members in a church where such signing is not practiced are in effect invited to the church where it is, even though that church may be of another denomination.

INSTITUTIONAL CARE

The church has created institutions for the care of persons with disabilities so serious as to make it painful and difficult for them to live in society. For the past one hundred-fifty years, it has been thought proper for the church to institutionalize such persons; in many cases the church has turned over to secular society the keeping of such institutions. Several of our denominations have been leaders in this work, which is motivated by humanitarian concern and often is necessary, although institutionalization is not always the best solution. The church in Germany helped create, both there and in this country through churches that follow their example, the idea that institutions can best take care of alienated people.

Such institutional care is big business in the churches in the United States and in West Germany. It continues in the German Democratic Republic where four of eight major rehabilitation centers for the sick and disabled are run by the church. In America directors add chaplains to the staffs of the institutions for the orphaned, elderly, handicapped, and retarded; others meet annually in a week-long symposium, sharing concerns and problems. There are a thousand chaplains of institutions, most selected within the context of rigorous training standards of clinical pastoral education.

Millions of dollars are provided by the churches in a noble attempt to care for persons of special need.

In the United Church of Christ, for example, 115 institutions are related to the church, several wholly owned. Twelve are hospitals, basically community in nature, some serving as the major hospital for a good-sized city. There are a dozen community and neighborhood centers of various kinds, another dozen units serve children, all the rest serve the aging. Two hundred thousand persons are served by sixteen thousand staffers at a cost of $250,000,000 in institutions valued at over $600,000,000. Remarkably, only $2,500,000 of this support money comes from the church and from individual church givers; all the rest is from the community, patients, or special grants.

The Episcopal Church, The United Methodist Church, and the three major Lutheran bodies each provide comparable data, reflecting the remarkable diversity of diaconal work in this country.

Churches which administer their own institutions also bring their expertise and experience into the secular community. Thus most of the major denominations in the United States have councils for health and welfare, designed not only to work with the health and welfare institutions operated by or related to the denominations, but also to relate the denominations to the varied secular institutional activities, thus keeping open the lines of communication between religious motivation and secular responses to need. All of this illustrates a marked difference from the diaconal service of churches elsewhere, particularly in West Germany.

BEGINNINGS OF "MISSION WITH"

At top hierarchical levels, both denominationally and ecumenically, the churches have recently groped toward expressing concern for the disabled in a mission with approach.

The Roman Catholic Church tried to say it in 1965 in the closing session of the Second Vatican Council. On the last day the Pope gave "a special word of recognition . . . to several groups in the human family." On hand to receive that word were government leaders, intellectuals, artists, women, workers, youth, and finally, two persons with physical impairments—a paraplegic and a blind man (Douglas Horton, *Vatican Diary* [Philadelphia: United Church Press, 1965].)

In the word "recognition" can we see the first outlines of a move from mission to to mission with? Perhaps not in the Council; but among some of the Protestant observers change might have been dimly seen. Certainly this writer remembers discussions of the marginalized with Dr. Lukas Vischer, head of the Commission on Faith and Order of the World Council of Churches, and a Protestant leader at Vatican Council II.

WORLD COUNCIL STATEMENTS

Perhaps the real first was the 1971 meeting in Louvain, Belgium, of the Faith and Order Commission of the World Council of Churches. Dr. Vischer came to Louvain with at least some memories of that Second Vatican Council. Add to this the deep personal feeling of staff member Dr. Gerald Moede, and the statement of concern for persons with handicaps was inevitable.

What should the Church do about these problems of isolation? 1. It should attempt to understand and to break down our fear of the handicapped and diseased and replace this fear with love and acceptance. 2. It should assert and defend their full humanity and seek to integrate them into the life of the Church. 3. It should support all movements to integrate them into society at large. 4. It should seek to discover and deal with new forms of isolation and marginalization. 5. It should recognize the right and need for militancy on the part of the handicapped as of other disadvantaged groups and recognize it not as a breach of human and Christian unity but as an attempt to enrich that unity. 6. The Church should recognize how easily it can become bourgeois, with its membership drawn from the active, successful, and healthy, and how often it tends to make membership difficult for the handicapped and the poor.

It is clear, however, that the Church has not fully taken account of this need; we must ask ourselves: Do we penalize the handicapped at the point of baptism, confirmation or communion, or admission to orders and offices in the Church? The churches should examine their practices to ensure that their treatment of the handicapped is indeed such as to manifest the nature of the Kingdom to men in the world. And they should make sure that it is not only doctrinally, but as fully as they are able in the life of our congregations. They should allow the handicapped and their needs to share in setting the tone of Church life, as they certainly did of Jesus' ministry. Their inclusion will influence the Church's worship in intercession, in forgiveness and absolution, a well as its architecture and physical facilities. The Church must not fail to recognize faith-healing and exorcism as forms of intercession directed to its healing ministry.[1]

Out of that conference, Dr. Vischer proposed a book on the unity of the Church and the handicapped in society, to show from the Church perspective the many meanings of persons with handicaps. Intended for publication in 1976, it came out three years later as *Partners in Life.*

At Nairobi in November 1975, the World Council of Churches adopted a resolution produced by Dr. Geiko Muller-Fahrenholtz, an associate of Dr. Vischer's on the World Council of Churches staff ("writing this statement is one of the proud achievements of my life"), which emphasized "ministry to *and with,*" and thus placed it squarely at the heart of the gospel. The concern had been set on the agenda with strong urging from a committee led by Miss Bette Knapp of New York. Her presence as a visitor to the Council, in her wheelchair, was a catalyst for adopting the resolution. Summary words from the resolution:

The Church's Unity includes both the "disabled" and "the able." A church which seems to be truly united within itself and to move toward unity with others must be open to all; yet ablebodied church members, both by their attitudes and emphasis on activism, marginalize and often exclude those with mental or physical disabilities. The disabled are treated as the weak to be served, rather than as fully committed, integral members of the Body of Christ and the human family; the specific contribution which they have to give is ignored. . . . The Church cannot exemplify "The full humanity revealed in Christ," bear witness to the interdependence of humankind, or achieve unity in diversity if it continues to acquiesce in the social isolation of disabled persons and to deny them full participation in its life. The unity of the family of God is handicapped where these brothers and sisters are treated as objects of condescending charity. It is broken where they are left out.

Some church groups in the United States had taken action even earlier: The United Methodist Church in the early 1960s brought into the curriculum of the church school a concern for persons with disabilities, and at its quadrennial General Conference in 1976 referred to its Board of Global Ministries a resolution looking toward churchwide expressions of concern for the handicapped. Several Lutheran bodies have had a long tradition of special ministries to such groups as the deaf and the blind, and the Episcopal Church has also been heavily involved in such specialized ministries.

HEALING COMMUNITY

Early in 1973 a number of church persons, along with experts from outside the church, created the Healing Community, an action-research project designed specifically to discover whether the Church really can respond to the various kinds of alienated persons in our society, and to define what some of these responses might be. It was intended to help the religious community facilitate the integration of the handicapped and the alienated into the mainstream of society and of local congregational life. Totally interdenominational and interfaith, Healing Community has been active both in this country and abroad. In the winter of 1973 it became administratively related to the New Samaritan Corporation of Connecticut and received major funding from the Lilly Endowment. Its current major goals include:

Creation of the caring congregation
Models of ministry with handicapped persons
Access to professional theological education

Consultants for independent living
Resource center for religious groups
International expansion of Healing Community
concept

Some of the most important findings of the action-research program are included in this book, and others have been published elsewhere. The Healing Community is one of many signs that a major ferment exists on the part of the churches expressing concern and on the part of that emerging minority who are asking whether only secular institutions will respond to their needs

DEINSTITUTIONALIZATION

But now, within our churches and in secular society, the process of deinstitutionalization is gathering force. For just one example, the number of persons in mental hospitals—over a half million, seven years ago—has been cut in half during the past six years. Most of our state governments and the United States Department of Health, Education and Welfare follow an intentional program of deinstitutionalization.

Within a stressful, technologically oriented society, the facts are clear. Ever more people are becoming alienated, and ever more of them are coming out into the open. A highly scientific Western world creates so much that is new and effective in medicine and technology that, on the one hand, more and more persons are injured and crippled by the use of that technology, but on the other hand, more persons severely injured are saved to live through technology. Thus we are creating and holding on to an ever-increasing number of handicapped individuals.

An overwhelming majority of these persons need not, should not, and indeed cannot be institutionalized. They are part of our society, not apart from it. More sharply than ever before, the idea of mainstreaming, keeping persons who differ from the norm within the main current of social life, is becoming a part of Western thinking. In this context there is an urgent need for society to respond to a coming-out party for those who are about to be deinstitutionalized, as well as a need for a far more adequate response to that much larger number who already are in our midst. Certainly the religious community, in its contact with people on every street corner and in every hamlet, has a prime opportunity to help in this mainstreaming process.

But the vast majority of handicapped persons are not in institutions. They are not in church either. They are the invisible people of our society, kept out of sight and out of mind. From the viewpoint of the church, as Bette Knapp reports:

Churchlife—at all levels—reflects the values and attitudes of the society in which it exists. Thus, in practice, it is reserved for those who are intellectually gifted, emotionally stable, and physically agile and mobile. The disabled, who individually may possess any combination of these attributes, are nevertheless looked upon as weak, helpless, incompetent, and unable to contribute. They are relegated to the sidelines or out of sight in caring institutions. They are placed in enforced situations of dependence, rather than helped towards self-actualization in life in the community. They are made objects of pity, condescension and charity, rather than accepted as colleagues and equals.[2]

How does the church keep them out? Architecturally, mostly inaccessible to persons in wheelchairs, the churches of our land defy the disabled woshiper to enter, in contrast to many secular buildings. In Las Vegas three years ago, in five different casinos, the writer asked five different persons in wheelchairs whether they had encountered any barriers to their entrance. The answer was always, "No, should there be?" Gambling casinos, O.K.! Churches, no!

How are churches overcoming these architectural barriers? The answer is by accident, by thoughtful concern of an individual member or a pastor, and by prodding from local and national groups.

The United Presbyterian Church in the U.S.A. in June 1977, sparked by a full year of work by the Healing Community's director in San Francisco, Dr. Norman Leach, declared a policy, "That all planning for new church buildings and/or major renovations to existing church buildings shall take into consideration the needs of the handicapped members of our society, in order that all may enter into our fellowship." Many pages follow, on site development, parking lots, ramps, entrances, doors, stairs, and rest rooms.

A week later, on Independence Day, July 4, ironically and happily the United Church of Christ called "each local congregation to take affirmative action assuring the full integration of persons with handicaps into membership of the Christian fellowship at all levels." It also urged the church to employ such persons, encouraged individuals with handicaps to become members of the ongoing life of the church, and specifically called attention to "removal of environmental and architectural barriers."

The National Council of Churches adopted in November 1977, that same year, a similar resolution asking for "necessary architectural modifications" and "overcoming attitudinal barriers."

Underneath all the statements about accessibility is the matter of attitudes. These barriers are most difficult to crack. Even definitions of the handicapped usually carry pejorative meaning not inherent in the actual disability.

Dean Krister Stendahl of Harvard University Divinity School declared, "One of the pains of being different is to have other people choose the way to classify us. To be defined by others is a kind of bondage against which all liberation movements should join, will join together." At the meeting sponsored by Mainstream of Riverside Church, the Lutheran scholar added, "Let not the world, or that part of the church which acts like the world, define you, but please define yourselves."[3]

The church therefore must go beyond the institutional response and move to a dramatic affirmation of congregational acceptance of the handicapped within the mainstream of congregational life. Congregational inclusivity is required, an inclusivity that implies the destruction of attitudinal barriers, that implies destruction of architectural barriers so that all may enter the house of God, and that involves a stance of advocacy for and with the handicapped.

These words of the writer were adopted by the World Council of Churches Consultation in Bad Saarow in April 1978.

A new day is dawning, a day of liberation, of self-awareness and pride. Facets of that many-splendored theme of freedom include the renewed feeling of self-identity and pride in that identity on the part of various groups in our society around the world, black and ethnic, women, and now persons with handicaps. This identity-consciousness may be seen as a response to a triad of human sin—racism, sexism, and handicappism. The sin in each case is the assumption by people of shortcomings or wrong inherent in the group criticized, whereas the error, indeed evil, is in the eye of the beholder. The white (or other group) creates racism; the male creates sexism; the so-called able-bodied person creates handicappism. Liberation can indeed lead to a new feeling of self-worth and proud identity.

Pressure from government itself is another reason churches are changing, since new laws mandate accessibility to public buildings. Thus, states, which define public buildings as those the public may enter, are now requiring church buildings, if they do major renovations, to include accessibility for persons with handicaps. With more and more states adopting such codes, church buildings may indeed change not from the moral imperative within the faith but from external requirements.

Partly from legal requirements, more from positive response to unity action, but most deeply from its theological and ethical imperatives, the church is beginning to say yes. A new day is dawning.

CHAPTER FIVE

The Marks of a Caring Congregation

FELLOWSHIP

A caring congregation expresses itself through the empathy of individual members. The empathy includes the ability to walk the very narrow line between swamping a newly bereaved or handicapped person with concern and affection and leaving him entirely alone out of fear of invasion of privacy or concern for our own embarrassment.

There is, of course, the prior or beforehand expression of the caring congregation: being open architecturally (ramps, accessible toilets), having some copies of the morning worship bulletin in Braille, and using sign language in one part of the nave or near the front). That open church is able to communicate its various programs and its space to the physically and sensorially impaired.

SETTING THE CONTEXT FOR FELLOWSHIP

A trinity of features marks the community of faith. Our earliest writings in the New Testament label them as follows: kerygma, the faith; koinonia, the fellowship; diakonia, service.

In each of these primary marks, concern for persons with handicapping conditions is integral and basic. They may not be separated out. The very fact that many Christians have placed ministry for handicapped individuals, the elderly, the physically disabled, the retarded, and so on, in one of these categories diakonia (service) has in effect created, or at least continued, a major aspect of the difficulty, that persons with handicaps and impairments are seen as recipients of service rather than as participants in the mission. It is when we separate out into one feature of the faith the concern for handicapped that we lose our basic rationale. We need to recognize all three aspects of the faith as we work with persons with handicapping conditions.

Look, then, at each of these distinguishing features in specific relationship to persons with impairment.

The first, what the Greeks called kerygma, is the faith. Saint Paul writes repeatedly of strength in weakness, and Jesus in his allusions to the Prophets, particularly Isaiah, and his statements of his own mission, sets the weakness of humankind at its very center, responding to God's grace to find our strength. The outcast, the maimed, the blind, and the lost are at the very center of our Lord's expression of this faith.

The proclamation of this faith is central to its reception. Therefore, insofar as a person with a physical impairment participates within this fellowship, he participates also in the proclamation of this faith. Insofar as she is part of the group selected by the Lord to receive that promise, so she must participate in relaying the word to the rest of humakind.

The koinonia, the fellowship, is the name for that warm, loving, and concerned group of persons who comprise the church. It includes all who receive God's gracious presence. It is the Body of Christ, people living together in love. It involves all of us, and we live it in a familial expression within the corporate body of the church. We are together in the joyous acceptance of God's grace. Recipients of the faith, we therefore live it out within the congregation, a living-out that expresses itself at worship on the holy days of the week and also in the fulfillment of the fellowship within the community.

THE FELLOWSHIP EXPRESSES ITSELF IN WORSHIP

Participation in oneship involves seeing, hearing, understanding, and responding. Since seeing is impossible for some persons, dependence upon auditory functions is critical, along with some such device as Brailling. For those with impaired hearing, sight is of critical importance, along with the translation involved with the use of sign language in at least one portion of the nave. Understanding what is going on may be difficult for the mentally retarded and the mentally impaired, so simplicity and clarity of the forms of worship are critically important. These facts lead to the question, Is uniformity in worship a requirement? Does everyone have to stand for singing? Does everyone have to maintain silence in some parts of the worship service? If the answers are yes, are persons in wheelchairs who are unable to stand for singing and the person with involuntary movements occasionally accompanied by sounds to be prevented from participation in worship?

The first thoughtless answer may very well be agreement that we do indeed have to stand for singing and that we do indeed have to maintain silence for some parts of the service. Yet we all have noted the individuals in every normal congregation who do not (can't?) "sing to the Lord"; they may stand but their lips remain sealed. Yet these people, some of whom may be pillars of the church, are never read out of the congregation. So why do we set up other demands for persons physically impaired or emotionally impaired?

The real answer is obviously no, we do not all have to stand for singing or to remain silent at some specific point. Unity in the Body of Christ does not necessarily mean rigid uniformity in worship.

It is not too late to escape the clutches of such rigidity in various aspects of church life and not just for the sake of more adequate inclusion of persons with handicaps. One theologian, P. T. Forsyth, has called the pew "the invention of the devil to keep people from hearing the gospel." Extending this comment, Martin Marty states: "The pew is a late innovation, an encumbering, committing, immobilizing piece of furniture that makes worship the act of looking at the backs of heads."[1]

It is not necessary that all the pews be straight. It may well be that chairs instead of pews may allow for considerably more flexibility in worship. A choir member with mobility problems does not have to process, but can take his or her place in the choir loft before the service begins.

Even the arrogance of the spoken word may become total. We who attend meetings abroad are already keenly aware of the arrogance of the English language so widely used in international conferences. But here is the arrogance of language itself, when words that may not be easily understood carry the basic message of God's saving grace. True, we are children of the Word, but the Word need not be expressed only in words. The sense of the sacred is critical, the involvement of the whole person, through sight and sound as well as in words. Such sense of the sacred is involved in the processional of the choir and the minister and in the beauty of the nave and chancel and sanctuary. It is expressed in artistry, in music, and in all other ways our ingenuity can fashion.

Precisely at this point of total bodily involvement Protestants may be jealous of their brothers and sisters in the Roman Catholic and Orthodox churches. There is a kind of sensuous richness in Orthodox worship particularly.

In a sense such use of worship forms appealing to all the senses is accidental in Protestantism; it is not usual in most Protestant forms of worship.

We recognize that the procession of the Cross, as in so many Episcopal churches, is a creator of the sense of the sacred for all of us and is critical for persons such as the mentally retarded. Preaching numbers of times in Church of Scotland congregations, the author was impressed with the practice of carrying the Bible in the procession and placing it on the pulpit. Furthermore, the practice, rediscovered during Vatican II, of carrying in the elements for the communion as an expression of the people, rather than having them mysteriously set in advance on the communion table, may be a sense of the sacred device we need to return to.

Would it not be ironic for the church, in moving toward a richer expression of the sacred because of a concern for providing new methods for the interiorizing of the faith for someone mentally retarded, to have that same faith be far more easily and deeply interiorized by the rest of the congregation! Again we have entertained angels unaware.

THE CHURCH AT STUDY

Centrality of the kerygma of the faith involves study of the same. Both Word and word demand of the congregation constant study of that faith in Scripture and in tradition.

For the handicapped, study of the Scriptures requires an intentional search for selections related to suffering, impairment, and loss. The implications of scriptural study must be brought out for us within the church. Thus, new readings and new insights may be gained from passages formerly directed in only one specific area. For example, the theme of unity and wholeness is seen in the third chapter of Galatians.

For in Christ Jesus you are all sons of God, through faith. For as many of you as were baptized into Christ have put on Christ. There is neither Jew nor Greek, there is neither slave nor free, there is neither male nor female; for you are all one in Christ Jesus. And if you are Christ's, then you are Abraham's offspring, heirs according to promise. [Gal. 3:26-29]

As followers of Christ, we are one body, but our unity is broken by the values of our society that intrude upon us and divide us. Such values emphasize our differences and make us blind to our oneness. They are responsible for the evils of racism, sexism, and classism. One of the most insidious evils is the separation imposed upon the physically and mentally disabled.

Many questions arise out of this passage and need response. Only a few such questions are listed; the reader will think of many more. Through faith we are all sons and daughters of God. Is that something we can believe? What makes it believable or unbelievable? Is the problem that God's acceptance of each of us is unbelievable? What is it about differences that makes us fearful and insecure? How do the values of our culture affect our attitudes about disability? Do we look on disability as the result of sin or punishment? Do we believe that it is divinely ordained for a particular purpose? How do we interpret Jesus' response to questions about disability? What attitude did he reflect in general?

Our study of the faith recognizes the prophets as a tutor for us, and Isaiah in the Suffering Servant passage that Jesus accepted for himself, is reaccepted by all of us in our suffering and anxiety. Jesus becomes our brother in suffering, even as he is our Savior in that suffering. The words Isaiah used are these:

> He was despised and rejected by men;
> a man of sorrows, and acquainted
> with grief;
> and as one from whom men hid their faces
> he was despised, and we esteemed
> him not. [Isa. 53:3]

Each of us, afflicted in some way, finds in the image of Christ as Suffering Servant the divine companion to our pain and separation. And our willingness to be servant, even in affliction, joins our life with his, giving it purpose, direction, and a common concern in love for all of humankind.

Here again questions arise. Some would be these: In what ways is the statement "everyone is handicapped" true? How does the process of aging imply disability? What does it mean to realize that we share affliction with Christ?

God's protection through his saving power is a recurring theme in Scripture:

> Yea, thou art my lamp, O Lord,
>   and my God lightens my darkness.
> Yea, by thee I can crush a troop,
>   and by my God I can leap over a wall,
> This God—his way is perfect;
> the promise of the Lord proves true:
> he is a shield for all those who take
>   refuge in him. [II Sam. 22:29-31]

"We suffered no harm, and we did not miss anything when we were in the fields, as long as we went with them; they were a wall to us both by night and by day" (I Sam. 25:15b-1a).

We discover, with Christ, that it is in our very weakness and affliction that we most dramatically experience the saving power of God, not only as a source of safety and refuge, but as an enabler in overcoming the obstacles in our path. Together with Paul we affirm, "My power is made perfect in weakness."

Often when we feel most alone, and most abandoned by God, we discover his saving love manifested through the acts of other people; often people we have perceived as unlikely instruments of God's ministry.

Even in our understanding of God's saving and protecting power, questions arise for study which explicate this faith.

Some people seem to have greater strength because of their affliction and/or disability; some are defeated by it. What makes the difference? On what basis does Paul claim that God's strength can work through our weakness? How do we translate this into the life of the church? Are we too action-, power-, and prestige-oriented? How much of our good works toward the poor, the handicapped, the victims of other forms of discrimination is humiliating to those we mean to help? How many times do we make the handicapped perform for us before we reward them for their afflictions? In what ways do we need to change in order for the handicapped to find it possible to share their talents within our Christian communities?

Study of the Scriptures brings forth the manifold witness made within that faith, the many-splendored thing it is. While the unity of the faith is one, the expression of that unity is fulfilled in countless ways:

To each is given the manifestation of the Spirit for the common good. To one is given through the Spirit the utterance of wisdom, and to another the utterance of knowledge according to the same Spirit, to another faith by the same Spirit, to another gifts of healing by the one Spirit. All these are inspired by one and the same Spirit, who apportions to each one individually as he wills. [I Cor. 12:7-9, 11]

It was a unique experience for the writer to see this transcendent "over the wall" experience in the German

Democratic Republic during the celebration of the 450th anniversary of the Reformation. Speaking within the Christian context, in meetings with a small group of the churches, the experience of the wall was totally transcended and suddenly all of us seemed to be in a universal place, defined by no boundaries at all.

The tragedy of walls that separate bodies within the whole church is that such division dissipates the power of Christ to reach out and serve the entirety of that world. Further, because of the wall, we cut ourselves off from the potential in each person to minister to as well as to be ministered unto. Also we cut ourselves off from the diversity of gifts to be found among all of us.

It is God who has placed us in this single body. "For he is our peace, who has made us both one, and has broken down the dividing wall of hostility" (Eph. 2:14).

It is Christ who makes us one, and as we are in him it is his love that becomes ours. It is a love so powerful that it destroys fear, hostility, and suspicion, and through it we are enabled to reach out with a new kind of freedom to those who are different as well as those who are the same.

SERVICE

"At the very time that the world is going to hell in a basket," stated the Episcopal layman William Stringfellow in a sermon at Grace Cathedral in San Francisco, in the autumn of 1975, "it is ironic to lift up any special ministry to individual persons in deep trouble. Yet, this is the central core of our faith." He underscored the very genius of Christianity as the personal response of binding up the wounds.

The whole religious community must fulfill intentionally and expertly the personal response of binding up the wounds, to respond to the need paraphrased above from Mr. Stringfellow's statement. That community also must look toward changing social structures so that both personally and structurally the community will respond to the needs of its alienated and handicapped members. To involve ourselves in the needs of alienated persons, we must commit our churches to creating models of religious community.

The message of salvation and wholeness, expressed and nurtured within the community of faith, is outwardly expressed in service. The kerygma, expressed through and nurtured within the koinonia, is expressed in diakonia. The message and the fellowship are fulfilled in service.

Diakonia, service, is thus the outward expression of the inner life of worship and study within the congregation. It is service to the world, fulfilled by the congregation, all of them, including persons with handicaps. This service to the world includes particular service to handicapped persons in institutions, for example, even as it also includes the mission and service of persons with handicapping conditions.

The World Council of Churches and the Christian Medical Commission based in Geneva voiced clearly this double approach of mission when it stated that the mission of the church, moving to mainstreaming persons with handicapping conditions, also recognized the continuing need to serve in institutional form particularly persons with varied special needs.

Thus, the picture of a servicing congregation, consisting of both handicapped and so-called nonhandicapped, serving the world is perhaps the unusual yet accurate picture of the true mission of the church. It truly portrays the diaconal service of the church, ministry with handicapped and ministry to handicapped.

Some of the service-marks describing a caring congregation are:

It is involved
It is committed to voluntary service
It fulfills a realistic appraisal of problems or programs
It shows concern for persons
It affirms the mainstream
It acts in advocacy
It acts on the factor of prevention
It seeks independence for all
It is an agent of change: changing attitudes
Its wounds are seen as part of its wholeness
It seeks healing
It focuses on unity
It works with partners in the secular community

The first mark, then, of a service-oriented congregation is by definition involvement. It is expressed in the quotation above from Mr. Stringfellow. It continues the flow of the river out into the ocean, not ending up in the Dead Sea with no outlet.

COMMITMENT TO VOLUNTEERISM

Volunteerism is a way of life in the United States. The church is a primary exponent of volunteerism, with literally millions of dollars provided free by church members in professional support, in administration, in teaching, in music, and in all the other activities of a local church. Add to this the outreach service to the community that church members volunteer to do in such institutions as Goodwill Industries, Easter Seal Society, and others, and we see the vague outline of an enormous social and economic factor in our society.

Such voluntary action may not be seen by most church people as the critically important element it really is. The author sees this disparity between the United States and most other Western countries regularly in chairing the Social Commission of Rehabilitation International, an organization with representatives from about thirty-five countries serving on its board. The constant assumption on the part of most members is that social concerns need to be filled primarily by the tax dollar and not by voluntary service.

What you as a church volunteer are doing has the double importance of the intrinsic value and its symbolic value.

REALISTIC APPRAISAL OF THE PROBLEM

Realistic appraisal—counting the cost, analyzing the various factors—expresses the third mark of service. It is to see the whole problem, or to examine as carefully as possible under the circumstances. The leap of faith is of course always necessary, but the prudent-man doctrine applies not only to classical economics but also to Christian service. We need to see the problem.

Finding out who are the handicapped in our midst is not simple. Many handicaps are hidden—a weak heart, a tendency to break bones, and other forms of the human situation that are genuinely difficult for the person but do not show on the outside. These hidden handicaps are many and varied, and millions of persons suffer, usually silently, within those bonds.

Another group of handicaps seems to be invisible, but show up suddenly in very embarrassing ways. Narcolepsy is a case in point. Here is a handsome young man with a distinguished air about him, yet he has gone through a dozen jobs in a dozen years. Now his wife, a nurse, supports the family because soon after he is on a job, he will fall asleep at some critical point, to the discomfiture and anger of his colleagues or bosses. He cannot help it. He may fall asleep at any moment, and he has no control over it at all. Medicine helps, but for this particular person, and there are many like him, a hidden handicap suddenly becomes extremely visible and embarrassing both to him and to others.

Still another of these handicaps that seems to be invisible becomes suddenly visible when we attempt to converse and discover that a person is deaf. Our responses are sometimes ludicrous. Rather than enunciating more clearly so that our lips can be read, difficult at best and impossible with the way so many of us slur our speech and mumble our words, we talk louder, wanting to force the individual to hear what we have to say. Then other people begin to look and blush, and we move away from this embarrassing situation as quickly as we can.

Many blind persons carry a walking cane to find the obstacle, step, or curb, so our response can be immediate to these persons. Still we do not know how to help or if our help is needed. Too often we attempt to guide the blind person by pulling rather than by giving our elbow for him to hold.

Then there is the individual in the wheelchair. She or he is very likely to be a young and handsome person, because spinal cord injury seems to hit especially the sports-minded, virile drivers of high speed cars or motorcycles. Or the "wheeler" may be past middle age, confined to wheels by some attack or chronic illness of advancing years.

Responding to a person in a wheelchair means that we are standing up and looking down on this individual, causing constraints. Usually it is difficult for us to bend down on one knee so that we are at the same height, so the constraint continues both in the wheeler and in ourselves. Further, the question of how we may help, especially if there is a series of steps involved as we are going up to the church, comes to mind. We do not know if we should specifically ask, or continue chattering about the weather.

One person in a wheelchair does not define the number. For that we need statistics. Data from the Rehabilitation Services Administration show that there are over 23 million disabled adults (persons between the ags of eighteen and sixty-four). That figure comprises all persons who are limited in kind or quantity of work, whether at a job or in the home. This is very close to one-fifth of the population in that age span. A second major group consists of children and youth (three to twenty-one years of age), disabled enough to require special educational provisions. The United States Office of Education states that these number 8 million. In spite of deinstitutionalization as a policy, there are over 2 million Americans of all ages who are institutionalized and disabled. All these figures add up to over 35 million Americans with various kinds of impairments.

Perhaps one-sixth of these 35 million have had their handicapping condition, their impairment congenitally; the rest became disabled during their lifetime.

Their numbers are increasing. Medical advances have now made it possible for a great majority of persons with severe spinal cord injury to continue a useful life instead of merely living. This is a far cry from what happened in the period during and following World War I when most such persons died within a few months or several years of the time of injury. Now, because of this medical science breakthrough, the span of life may be quite considerable. Life expectancy according to a recent report in *The New York Times* has now gone up to seventy-one years. A great many more disabilities and illnesses may express themselves. For those congenitally disabled, the numbers increase sometimes radically because of the increase in infant care. A dramatic case in point is the rapidly rising incidence of spina bifida, a congenital disability. With new operations and new kinds of care available the child has a much better chance of living. The older group mentioned above is increasing proportionately within the population, so that by the end of the next decade these people will number one-fifth of the population.

Even today we recognize our society as an interdependent one, with some people routinely caring for others in the body politic. Most young people are students until age eighteen, and a great many are students, and continue to be supported primarily by others, until age twenty-five or thirty. Unemployment insurance provides for a portion of the population during certain luckless periods in their lives. It is in a sense no surprise to us then to realize that within perhaps fifteen or twenty years the number of all such persons (disabled, institutionalized, unemployed, and retired will comprise almost the same number as breadwinners.

Realistic appraisal, of which these few pages are a tiny speck, is a critical requirement in service.

SHOWING CONCERN FOR THE PERSON

Figures and statistics are not enough. Showing concern for the individual, his feelings, hopes, and aspirations, is another mark of the caring congregation in its service to the community. Showing concern involves appreciation for the feelings and attitudes of individuals, how they feel about themselves and how they define themselves, an ability to see their situation as they see themselves exhibit it.

Let us look briefly at some of the meanings of the words used to describe persons with handicapping conditions: handicapped, crippled, impaired, infirm, sick, ill, invalid, afflicted, deformed, deaf and dumb, living in darkness, suffering from, something wrong with, confined to a wheelchair, wheelchair bound, wheelchair victim, crutch user, Tiny Tim, cripple, deafmute, retard, victim.

Is it possible to develop a whole new positive terminology in which a person is perceived without a handicap, but experiences a handicap in certain situations? This handicapper may then be more adequately defined, in terms of characteristic only, as a wheelchair user, even a charioteer, or worker or operator from a wheelchair. Even Tiny Tim can become Terry Terrific or Tiger Tony.

By the same token, most of us should be recognized for what we are, "Tabs," temporarily able-bodied.

Perhaps even in our social relationships we should work not with barrier-free design but "harmonious design for all," or "equal design consideration," thus recognizing our concern is for all people, not simply some 2 million wheelchair users.

Identity is a two-way street. You will have noted perhaps that some of your handicapped acquaintances see themselves as persons without real identity, certainly in many cases without gifts usable by others. Perhaps the experience of one young woman, severely cerebral palsied, would be of help. LeAnne Nelson writes of hearing a verse from Paul's Letter to the Romans at a Bible camp for handicapped adults, "Having gifts that differ according to the grace given to us, let us use them" (12:6). After her first astonishment, thinking that God could not possibly think that these handicapped adults had gifts, she thought more about the ways a disabled person can provide help for others. She said, "Our attitude towards life and towards others reflects our love of God. A cheerful attitude can be like a ray of sunshine." She also recognized that the human voice can be augmented by silent prayers on behalf of others. Other gifts arose in her mind and she now thanks God for "giving me hidden gifts." Perhaps the "gift of an unbroken spirit is one of the most helpful of all."[1]

Our defenses against seeing the person whole seek psychological and theological support; the two are often tightly intertwined. We set up answers for not attempting to deal with persons who are different, and therefore do not include them in our own culture, common life, and personal interaction.

To allege even to ourselves that he or she is subhuman is no longer an acceptable way of dealing with physically or mentally handicapped persons. Even the idea of being a menace to the very structure of our society can no longer be easily accepted. But to be able to assume sickness is still widely present, even though, of course, most persons with handicapping conditions are not sick. This is a physical or mental condition, sometimes changing radically, improving or worsening, but the actual illness is one thing, and the handicapping condition is another. Deal with the two separately.

When people refer to "your special child," "your eternal child," "this holy innocent," they describe a theological-psychological attempt to deal with the abnormal, especially in children. Reflecting a centuries-old tradition of response to handicapped persons, these words reflect our desire to avoid this situation. If the person is already a holy innocent, what need is there for us to do something about him? Why do we need to involve her in our daily living? This idolatry makes it impossible for us to fulfill a ministry either to or with such persons. If they are already in some heavenly place, they need no help from us.

AFFIRMING THE MAINSTREAM

Mainstreaming is another mark of the caring society. We have come to recognize this, through litigation particularly, as a right for the disabled child to have an education. Many books and monographs have been written on various aspects of mainstreaming in education. But mainstreaming for all persons is a mark of the caring society, the acceptive quality of society that assures the deviant individual that she or he is truly a part of the community. Such recognition may not miss, must not, the potential resource of one-tenth of the population. There are far too many persons with opportunities for creative expression in employment, in the arts, in the humanities, and in the simple business of being human, for us to refuse to accept that value.

We recognize also in the pluralistic society from which most of us come that there are many varied and rich resources from all kinds of people who are different from the norm in the society. Acceptance into the mainstream comes out of seeing the many-splendored thing that our society is. The concept of the utilization of all resources is also part of the response of a caring society. Here is a resource that can and must be used.

Such mainstreaming, such social acceptance of persons with handicaps, may also arise out of the sense of interdependence we hold as a common goal. It is the sense of grace that individuals offer and that society then may accept. We are able to rest more easily with our own finitude as we see the ways in which literally thousands of individuals have surmounted difficulties and have offered to all of us a new sense of the grace that is the basis of a good society.

ACTING IN ADVOCACY

Acting in advocacy is another mark, recognizing the right of the person with the disability to be involved in her own self-advocacy, to do his own thing. He need not be constantly the object of our mission but participate in the common mission of the church along with the rest of us. It is advocacy *for,* of course, but even more it is advocacy *with.*

To permit and to encourage self-advocacy by and for the diasbled is one of the marks of a concerned society. It is not that we do something for them, rather we grant them the dignity of doing something for themselves. That means being involved in decisions affecting them.

At the Menninger School of Psychiatry, a hospital charting system was drawn up with the hierarchy totally shifted. Instead of the senior psychiatrists at the top, the patient was at the very center, and his relationships with members of the staff were shown in what was essentially a pie chart. To repeat: you know what is good for the handicapped, but unless that person is totally involved in the decision-making, likely he will not be able to fulfill the process.

We are the ones who are concerned about liberation. We, all of us together, are concerned about the identity of the person and the wholeness of the individual. In this recognition we are freed and liberated, free to attain, within justice, our ultimate potential.

Advocacy includes participation, placing ourselves within the group seeking its rights. Just as mission *to* the handicapped becomes mission *with* the handicapped, so advocacy asserts partnership.

ACTION ON PREVENTIVE FACTORS

Joe Doe's scarred face, resulting from a car crash in which he was hit by a drunken driver, is a permanent psycho-social barrier for him. Now twenty-nine years old, he will have fifty-two years in a normal life-span to live with this disability. He was just one of 720,000 persons *beyond* those routinely seriously injured in car crashes in 1978. These three-quarter-million persons comprise an *additional* number, beyond the accepted number routinely injured in automobile accidents during the past year.

Jane Doe died last year at age forty-one, of emphysema. She had been a heavy smoker for a decade and a half, including two periods when she was pregnant, with resultant functional brain loss for both of the children born in those periods. Jane Doe should have lived to age seventy-eight. She died thirty-one years earlier, after producing two children who will have real quality of life problems for themselves and will be responsible for major economic loss to the American community.

Henry Roe died last week at age twenty-seven. He had a serious birth defect that both his parents knew would happen. The pediatrician had warned them that there was a 90 percent chance the child would be born with that particular syndrome. The parents opted against any kind of action about genetic counseling except the action of having a child.

Why are the churches so silent about alcohol? About tobacco? Why are the churches silent about the money spent for guns and war planes that could be spent for health? Why are the churches mute on nuclear arms proliferation? Why are there so few words about genetic counseling?

The Christian Medical Commission in Geneva, co-operating with a number of church bodies, stated: "Action for prevention of disability is a critical demand not only for secular governments but also for the church." They added: "The World Health Organization and Rehabilitation International estimate that approximately 400 million to 450 million human beings around the world are seriously handicapped in various ways, and more than half of these disabilities could be prevented by overall preventive measures."

SEEKING INDEPENDENCE FOR ALL

Accepting and urging independence for other persons is another mark of the caring group. Independence has important economic benefits in society as well as those accruing to the individual because of his or her new-found freedom. Since his independence may make it possible for him to work all day at a job instead of being confined at home, he is not only earning wages for himself but also returning money to society in terms of taxes.

An example is an amputee who takes a job as a purchasing agent with an annual salary of $12,500. Because of her accident she could have received higher annual benefits in insurance, public aid, Social Security, and workmen's compensation in the amount of $5,616. Now, on the job, her estimated annual federal and state income taxes and Social Security is $3,000, so that the annual gain to society (taxes plus prior benefits) is $8,616. The projected gain to society by age sixty-five will be $267,096. A quarter-million-dollar benefit to society, entirely separate from the human value involved.

Robert Armaroli, placement specialist at the Rehabilitation Institute of Chicago, says that studies show handicapped people are excellent workers, that absence rates are equal or lower, that insurance rates do not increase, that job turnover is exceptionally low, and that only minimum accommodations are necessary (Chicago *Tribune,* September 19, 1976).

AN AGENT OF CHANGE

As change agents in society, changing highly negative attitudes toward the handicapped into more positive ones, the church expresses its possibilities for being truly a caring group.

Changes in attitudes are made with enormous difficulty. In *The New York Times* for August 22, 1975, Dr. Robert Kleck reported on the difficulties encountered by handicapped and nonhandicapped persons when they meet. He states that the stigma of disability tends to dominate the relationship between the handicapped and nonhandicapped persons, and that until the stigma is removed the meeting will be emotionally charged. Dr. Kleck suggests that handicapped and nonhandicaped be honest and true to their own feelings.

To be a change agent, you in the church must have credibility, some influence, a desire to make changes, and a willingness to make changes in your own self. Perhaps spending some time in a wheelchair may cause a dramatic change within yourself and therefore within another. As we move from anxiety and our fear about ourselves being disabled to understanding the nature of the disabilities and their problems, we can then make positive changes in our own and other persons' attitudes. Further, "messages that stress similarities between disabled and non-disabled people, emphasizing the cnvironmental and situational difference, may prove effective." Here the power of positive thinking is required.

Professor John Jordan, while at Michigan State University, showed conclusively in a cross-cultural study of attitudes that real change took place at the point where there was identification with the individual with a handicapping condition. This means that putting the best foot forward on the part of the person with the impairment is a requirement. Consider again the strategies suggested at the close of the previous section on advocacy.

THE WOUNDED HEALER

A congregation gathered one Sunday after worship to deal with the alcoholism of its minister who had been hospitalized. Led by a neighboring pastor and by several of their own members who were recovering alcoholics, members of the congregation poured forth their sense of care and concern for their pastor, stating, "We will not sit in judgment of our pastor, but will instead take him back when the hospitalization is ended." The appreciation was genuine; the love was highly evident at almost a tearful level. But there was an underlying thread that assumed he would come back cured, whole, ready to begin again the task of being the spiritual leader of the congregation and as such the one who could do no wrong. He would be totally whole.

The human being does not live like that. We live in fragments, in tension, in anxiety. The minister brings to every task the situation from which he or she comes. The congregation seeing the fact of this tension and difficulty in its own life ought to be able to project that for the spiritual leader as well. It is in weakness, says Paul, that we become strong. Our help for others, as that of minister for parishioner, comes out of human weakness so that God's own strength can be glorified. "Wounds are the occasion where God intimates his own creation," wrote Professor Henri Nouwen of Yale, and Morton Kelsey adds, "God sends the wound, God is the wound; God is the wounded. God heals the wound." Robert Raines says it in beautifully poetic image: "Health is a matter of wholeness and not perfection. Health has to do with being real and offering our sins, mistakes and brokenness as multicolored threads to be woven into a rich tapestry of humanity by the healing grace of God."

The wounded healer is a concept which grows naturally out of the preceding way of looking at a total society. The person may recognize that healing comes not only from a clear intellectual understanding of a problem, presented in the most sophisticated of language and media, but also from the simple sharing of common backgrounds. All of us have known this special help provided by the wearer of our own moccasins, by the one who has gone through the same valley.

Scripture caps for us the idea of the wounded healer.

Dr. Karl Menninger has written persuasively about this concept, calling it "weller than well." Many persons are cited to show how their response to a sorrow, a rebuff, an illness, an impairment somehow made it possible for them to fulfill for society and for themselves much more than was lost through the impairment.

A healing community, a caring society, does not come into being by accident. It comes at cost, intentionally creating a binding together, an acceptance of disparate units, a regularly celebrated remembrance of its part, and a stated assurance for the future, a concern for one another, and an appreciation of both the wholeness and the separateness of the society. All of this is the kind of integument that we utilize in creating the community.

IT SEEKS HEALING

The churches cannot and may not escape their responsibility for preventing and binding up the wounds of humanity. Powerful motives urge us to action.

Christianity affirms that life is one; it symbolizes the essential unity of life.

Christianity carries the hope and assurance of healing; it is the vessel of God's grace.

Christianity expects the kingdom of God; it makes the demand for peace, compassion, and justice.

Religion deals with the totality of life and with the whole person. It knows the human striving toward wholeness. "We are not at rest until we find rest in thee," said St.

Augustine. Christianity has a special concern for persons who have been broken and become alienated from themselves, from society, and from God.

FOCUSING ON UNITY

Beyond logic is faith. Beyond an orderly outline is a word of reconciling love. Beyond our equitable and fair pattern is an act of divine giving. God's act of love for humankind, in Christ, is the ultimate answer to healing, for healing is seen as salvation, as wholeness, as a new unity transcending the old. It is that unity we note in God's plan for the world. Paul states it in his letter to the Christians in Ephesus:

Now he has let us in on the secret of his plan, which is to make Christ head over everything, both spiritual and material. He'll do this in his own good time, when he thinks things are right. And it has already been determined at "headquarters," from which come all directives that get things moving, that we who have put our trust in Christ shall take part in this plan and be a credit to the cause.

You all, too, when you listened to the message of the truth, the good news of a "new way of walking," and put it into action, then the promised Holy Spirit put his OK on you. This is our "certificate of membership," entitling us to engage in the liberation movement set up for God's glory.

This is why, when I heard about your Christian living and the love you show towards everybody in the fellowship, I couldn't stop thanking God for you all every time I prayed. And I asked the God of our Lord Jesus Christ, our glorious Father, to give you spiritual wisdom and a better understanding of him. May he give clear sight to your soul's eyes. May you know the hope which his call inspires and the wonderful resources available to Christians because of their membership in his family. May you experience the incredible outburst of his power in us who rely on his might and his abundant energy. This same energy working in Christ raised him from the dead and gave him spiritual victory and authority over every ruler and every governor and every judge and every sheriff and every other title you can name both now and in the future. Furthermore, it brought everything and everybody under his rule, and made him the head of everything in the fellowship, which is his body, the full expression of him who gives meaning to everything everywhere. [Eph. 1:9-23 *The Cotton Patch Version of Paul's Epistles*][2]

CHAPTER SIX

Getting Started: Organizing for Action

Three approaches for the implementation of our task, that of making our churches attitudinally and architecturally accessible, are necessary.

The first approach sets the context of organizational development, the way things get done, outlines the guiding force of the person who looks behind the scenes in order to accomplish a goal. This approach is a must for the fulfillment of the goal and recognizes the real facts of life in congregations, namely that the president of the church or pastor is not necessarily the one whose word finally determines whether or not a program is accepted by the congregation.

The second approach is a one-two-three series of statements, providing the overview and the listing of tasks that need doing.

The third approach is a work-sample, applying to a specific congregation the procedures suggested in the first approach and the goals of the second.

ORGANIZING THE APPROACH WITHIN THE CONGREGATION

We know that change occurs within the local congregation through the action of the Holy Spirit within that congregation. We also know that changes occur when a carefully thought-out and highly motivated process is presented within the congregation and before its people.

At the beginning the leader recognizes the need for a change in the congregation in order that new attitudes might be developed and that architectural access might be implemented. *Seeing the need is the first step.* At this point the leader alone, but preferably with two or three other individuals, works through the following steps in order to enlist the aid of other leaders within the congregation and finally to implement their concern.

The second step is to define what is wanted. What change do you want in your congregation? What in particular, in specifics, do you want to change? You need to be very clear what it is that you wish to accomplish. You have to do more than go to the minister and say, "I want First Church to accept people with handicaps and to change its architecture." Prepare a *written, specific list* of the changes to be made, the only generality being the goal. All the rest will be specific objectives.

You may design such specific objectives, for yourself and your ad hoc committee. List goals for the committee on architectural accessibility, or committee breaking down the wall of negative attitudes toward the handicapped, or changing our attitudes: accepting the handicapped in the life and witness of the church, or access to all, in mind and in building. Whatever the group is called it has several tasks:

1. To recognize its dual task: architectural and attitudinal accessibility
2. To work *with* persons with handicaps, listening to their feelings and concerns
3. To work *with* the minister in a Sunday morning consciousness-raising experience
4. To work through the church school staff to create opportunities, such as simulations of handicaps, for the students
5. To create similar "simulation" experience for persons within the church, to be related to some church fair or other function when a lot of people can see what is going on, or to be held at a very private level
6. To work with the worship committee to discover ways in which persons with various kinds of physical or sensory handicapping conditions are excluded by the present forms of worship
7. To develop a study theme on attitudinal barriers for education groups for the young people and adults

The third step, taken before presenting this list to the minister or other church leaders, is to determine who are the movers and shakers, if you do not already know this. Then, from your knowledge of the system, set up the procedure you want to follow in getting the job implemented. Remember, you are not seeking the martyrdom of saying, "I tried, but it didn't work." You are seeking the implementation of a task that will bring into the church, and help bring into the mainstream of society, a potential ten percent of the congregation. This major task is one requiring all your finesse and strategic knowledge. You need to know the rules in the congregation, beginning with the written rules, the construction and by-laws, and going on to the unspoken ones, often more powerful than the written ones. Where are these centers of authority in your church? Part of knowing the territory is to see the negatives and the positives in potential congregational action and to list them.

The fourth step is for you to note the factors in effecting change in the persons involved. The process for you to utilize is described graphically. Take a sheet of paper and draw a line down the center. On the left-hand side list the persons and the factors within the congregation you feel would be helpful to your proposal.

The positive factors might include the following:

Henry Henrickson wants to be known as avant-garde in both the church and the community and can latch on to something like this with vigor.

The Petersons' seventeen-year-old daughter has been using a wheelchair for two years, and never comes to church with her parents.

Mr. Holland, an architect, gives generously to the church, but has never been aked to do anything in his field for the congregation.

Next on the right-hand side of the paper, list persons and factors that may be negative to the cause:

John Jones is always opposed to any expenditure for anything in the church.

Harry Lord is concerned about what other churches may think about what First Church does and usually worries about it.

The minister's wife tends to be concerned about new expenditures because of what it might do to the possibility of a raise in her husband's salary.

First Church is on the Historical Landmarks listing, and no change may be made except with the approval of the commission.

ANALYZING THE FACTORS

The fifth step for you and your co-workers is to analyze each of the positive and negative factors you listed. On the matter of landmark status, how easy is it (or difficult) to get that commission to make changes? What approach to Mr. Lord's ego can you make? The process here is the specific pointing to factors and to individuals, determining the best strategy.

If one of the negative factors is the statement, "We haven't had a person with a handicap in church since last Christmas," maybe you and the minister need to take a careful look at the membership of the church to determine how many persons you think have some kind of disability. You also need to determine how often those persons have attended church over the past few years. "You need to know the territory" is part of the Bible of the salesman, and since you are selling a new approach within the congregation, you have to know the territory of this congregation. You need to know what First Church is really like in its entire demography.

It is highly likely that the minister, church secretary, or others with whom you speak about the matter may initially think that there are no handicapped persons within the congregation, or two or three at the most. A careful review of the congregation, however, may reveal that there is a large number who are related to the congregation through families or who live in the parish area. Finding the names is an informal process; it is not a census. Any listing of names should be done privately on yellow paper, perhaps only scribbled and certainly not copied and passed around as First Church's handicapped list.

Concerning some persons who are probably negative, you need to have the data to respond to their fears or objections. You may not convert them, but you may neutralize them. However, in dealing with them always respect their position and see them as human beings, not as pawns in your game.

KEEPING IT ON THE FRONT BURNER

The sixth step is to keep it going. You will continue to push for meeting and strategy sessions. You will continue to meet with individuals; you will continue to provide resources for the individuals working in your cause. You will provide information and additional referral where necessary. You will keep the pot boiling. This does not mean that you personally must do all these things. You will enlist others and enable others. As many persons as possible should be involved. Often unanticipated developments may be wondrous for the cause.

Keep enlarging constantly that resource list of media helps, of persons, of organizations. Surely one of the worst things we can do is to say that something ought to be done and then provide no personal, fiscal, or organizational resource to back up our contention and hope. Enlisting someone in a cause means you give backup data and emotional support along the way.

At some point near the middle of the process, or earlier, depending on your judgment, you may send out a questionnaire to members of the congregation. A sample follows, which *must* be changed to fit your own congregation. Questions may be added, some deleted.

I. Questions for discussion within the religious community
   A. Pastor, priest, or rabbi
      1. Have you been studying Scripture with reference to the handicapped and alienated?
      2. Have you been reading and disseminating other documents recently published? (Resources are available.)
      3. Have you written to your ecclesiastical headquarters about your concern in this area, secured their materials, and offered suggestions as to how your congregation has responded?
   B. For the outreach committee or Board of Deacons
      1. How are you dealing with the comment "We don't have anyone crippled or in wheelchairs"?
      2. What have you done about the listing of the various kinds or architectural barriers within the church?
      3. How have you dealt with expressions that say in effect, "We really don't want these people in our church"?
      4. How have you responded to other attitudinal barriers?
   C. For the Education Committee
      1. How have you worked this concern into the curriculum?
      2. Have you done simulation programs, with persons with handicaps, for the young people?
      3. What other ways have you developed the curriculum to deal with this concern?
   D. For the Board of Trustees
      1. How did you deal with cost concerns on a new ramp?
      2. Did you search out other opinions?

3. Did you compare the cost of renovating over against the contributions of persons newly able to come to church?
4. Have you recognized the safety factors inherent in ramps over against the steps for most of the church population?

II. Listing of changes already fulfilled in your congregation
   A. In architectural accessibility
   B. In worship
   C. In religious education
   D. In theological understanding
   E. In advocacy programs outside the congregation

III. Additional follow-up or implementation needed
   A. In getting into the building
   B. In congregational life and expression
   C. In psychological and theological discussions
   D. Other

The foregoing is a specific device for focusing attention. Another such device—a consciousness-raising experience—is the celebration of "Access Sunday."

Many churches during 1979 set aside a particular Sunday as Access Sunday. Originated by Healing Community, the idea spread throughout churches around the country. Inside the Sunday morning bulletin was a specific little flier, designating "Access Sunday" as a time for the church to:

Take a new look at the contributions of the handicapped
Validate the life and witness of the handicapped in the Christian community
Remind the congregation that the church's unity includes both the disabled and the able
Demonstrate anew the wholeness of the family of God
Affirm continuing need for institutional care where

necessary and also to call for congregational acceptance of the handicapped within the mainstream of church life
Begin structural changes so that all may enter
Study and act upon attitudinal barriers in the people of the church.

Bulletins continue to be available from the Healing Community office in New York, with a full flier, inside pages offering quotations for possible procedures, and a brief listing of resources.

The pastor of a West Coast church put it this way: to proclaim "Access Sunday" is an occasion to—

1. Roll out the welcome mat for all persons including the handicapped
2. Back up the welcome with an actual invitation (transportation)
3. Celebrate removal of any remaining architectural barriers to access by handicapped persons
4. Pray for removal of any remaining attitudinal barriers to access by handicapped persons
5. Celebrate the church as a healing community
6. Strengthen our advocacy role and our monitoring of legislation to aid the handicapped

He then stated that "instead of a questionnaire we invite your report of positive achievement or intention on any or all of the above items."

A SAMPLE APPROACH

Now that we have understood more clearly the approach of management or organizational development (working through the system, recognizing the realities of the power structure within the local organization) let us take a specific task and go through all the steps necessary to get the job done.

First, we define our task, our overall goal. The goal is to make the church architecturally accessible and attitudinally open to persons using wheelchairs or crutches. Our example is St. Stephens Church, in a Midwestern city, built thirty-five years ago with nine lovely steps in front. St. Stephens is a handsome stone structure but seems to have no way of providing for architectural accessibility.

Armed with your knowledge of organizational development and your listing of the steps that need to be taken in making St. Stephens have in effect no steps, you first seek out a member who uses a wheelchair and you listen to him. "When I first came back from rehabilitation after my automobile accident, I wanted to resume life in the community as I had known it before. I was a member of the choir at St. Stephens so twice a week I came to church for choir practice and for Sunday morning worship. In each case, two husky guys from the bass section helped me up those steps. Sometimes I wanted to get there early to practice my part with the organist, but I was always afraid that no one would be around to help me up those steps. Also, I wanted to be able to get in on my own. I felt demeaned in a way in being carried up all the time." While this demeaning aspect is of critical importance there is also the simple matter of danger involved. Many persons do not know how to carry a person in a wheelchair up a flight of nine steps.

As you talk with John you recognize that he is in no great hurry to make changes, and although he may well be the symbol you need to make St. Stephens accessible, he may not actually be an active ally for you. You see him as a tremendous symbolic support, but no pusher. In fact, John's feelings remind you that persons with diabilities are not all alike, they are different from one another, they do not necessarily present similar feelings, and they do not all present a united front on breaking down barriers. They are individuals, like the rest of us.

You turn then to two new members of the church, both of whom are contractors. You ask them if they would be willing to provide the direction and the materials for the creation of a ramp in order to make St. Stephens more accessible. On their hearty yes, you go back to the Board of Trustees and state that there is an offer of free oversight and wholesale cost on materials, and you again point out that John needs to be carried up those stairs to his danger and discomfiture and to the difficulty of persons who are not really all that strong. Members of the Board of Trustees promise that something will be done soon.

Your next visit is to the architect who knows the standards of the American Institute of Architects. With these in hand, you spend an hour or so with him going over potential places for a ramp or other place of easy ingress into the church. The architect has strong recommendations as to the best possible place, including a guide for replanting trees in order that the original design of the church might still show clearly even with a ramp at the side. You go then to the pastor with this information, coupled with the offer of the two new members to provide material at cost, and their leadership in the building of the ramp. The figure suggested is approximatey one thousand dollars.

By this time you have in effect created a committee on architectural accessibility, composed of John in the wheelchair, two new members who are contractors, an architect who is ready to serve, and the minister who is ready to listen and utilize resources.

Before you go to the Board of Trustees members again, you review your statement. It should be simple and short. A copy of it and a packet of backup informational material should be available for each trustee.

Your statement does not say that you wish to replace steps. You say, "We want steps and an alternative to steps." You say, "We want to make the building accessible to John, and we think that at the same time it will be made much easier for a great many other members of the congregation."

A member of the Board of Trustees points out that no congregational meetings are necessary for expenditures under one-thousand dollars. Elated, you dash back to the contractors to see whether this thing can really be done for under one thousand dollars, and after a short pause you get such assurance. As a result, the Board of Trustees acts on the basis of a proposal from a number of members, a positive statement from the Board of Outreach, your presentation to them, and the affirmation on the part of the minister. A relatively few members of the church have actually led the way.

FINDING PARTNERS IN SECULAR SOCIETY

We are not alone; our churches are set within a sea of community organizations, all potential partners in the common task of creating a caring society. Seek them out. Find the contacts. Learn the ropes. They are often within the church walls.

Agencies abound. The list would include the Y.M.C.A.,

the Y.W.C.A., the Council of Churches, parents' groups for retarded children and others with mental retardation, local units of voluntary health organizations, such as Easter Seal, Goodwill, Volunteers of America, religious organizations with particular community outreach, the Salvation Army, tax-supported welfare groups, organizations for the blind and other specific groups, ethnic organizations, and many more.

CHAPTER SEVEN

Done-Yet Not Done

"When thou hast done, thou has not done," wrote John Donne in that haunting double meaning, "for I have more." For all of us there is more, more to fulfill, to create, to seek, and to find. You will find this true in your voluntary service in helping create a caring congregation, a healing community. You have done so much, yet "temples still undone o'er crumbling walls their crosses scarcely lift." We need to provide the love to raise the broken stone, the creative hearts to "bridge the human rift".[1]

Your achievement in helping your local church move toward that healing community open to and with persons with varied disabilities is one in which you can rejoice. You note the many forms this achievement takes in churches around the land.

Now your organization has taken place. You may have followed some of the guidelines suggested in this book. You may have developed your own, following your own intuitions. "Do it your way" has been a guiding principle for us, based on our recognition of the many kinds of expertness and strengths available in the religious community.

Examples of that community exist widely over the country. Most of those mentioned below have come out of activity within Healing Community, but some have simply been Spirit-led. We can rejoice in the wide front on which we are currently engaging the forces of exclusion and segregation.

Early in 1974 a survey by Healing Community indicated that less than half of one percent of the congregations in St. Louis were accessible to persons in wheelchairs, this accessibility taken as a criterion for genuine accessibility. After concerted attack upon the problem, with primary support from the Danforth Foundation, dozens of congregations were involved in a four-year program that is still going on. A survey a year ago showed that over one percent of the churches were now accessible—a gain of one hundred percent in several years. But note: that gain is within the context of a tiny fraction of the total congregations in the area. The work has barely begun.

A carpenter at a suburban church unit has built ramps in homes for inner-city residents as well as for suburban church members. Recently he liberated a young boy who had been housebound by building a simple but effective ramp for him.

The educational departments of four churches have included course materials on the impact within the church community of persons with physical or emotional disabilities.

Numbers of churches have arranged dialogue sessions between persons with disabilities and various church or synagogue committees and workshops, reports the Indianapolis group.

Two dozen ministers have preached sermons on the handicapped and alienated. "We can minister to lost sheep because we are in a real sense lost sheep!"

A southern Illinois congregation reports an increased awareness of needs of the handicapped to which the church has responded in a visitation program and the beginning of signing sermons for the deaf.

Numbers of churches report that when they make their churches architecturally accessible, there is an immediate ripple effect on nearby churches. Also within the congregation there is an effect in terms of attitudinal barriers.

Many churches report that they are building ramps and reworking washrooms to provide architectural access for persons with disabilities. A number of persons add that the attitudinal barriers are higher than the architectural ones.

A theological seminary in one of the cities points up the architectural problems: "Besides building ramps and chairlifts, we find major structural problems to overcome, and we'll do it! In the meantime, the new library is accessible, and some classes have been moved there to accommodate wheelchair students."

A church in southern Illinois altered the doors of the restrooms so they would be accessible for persons with physical handicaps. They are now working to get a chairlift for the church and for the fellowship hall.

Two parishes and a synagogue have developed policy statements affirming the responsibility of the religious community to extend outreach to persons disabled and otherwise handicapped.

There are three hundred thousand men out of Vietnam

who bear physical wounds of that war, in many cases wounds that will be with them to their graves.

Memorial Day calls us to honor those who died. Perhaps even more so we should remember those who gave of themselves, were wounded, and continue to live in a society that refuses to honor them. There are almost eight hundred thousand Vietnam veterans with less than honorable discharges, and there are a disproportionately high number of Vietnam veterans in prison, according to the National Veterans Law Center in Washington, D.C.

Models of ministry with the disabled have been a particular concern, out of Healing Community discussions, for Foothill Congregational Church in Los Altos, California. This church developed a self-help housing program for the physically disabled. The Reverend Charles Bezdek and lay leaders made this a unique and inspiring program demonstrating how a congregation may minister to and with the disabled.

Shiloh United Church of Christ in Danville, Pennsylvania, recognized that its congregation was demographically older and included numbers of persons with walkers and crutches. With the options before them, they chose the accessibility route, and intalled an elevator in the section between the old building, which included the nave on a second floor, and a new section, which included the fellowship hall classrooms. The elevator now makes the church truly accessible. The celebration service was based on the story in the Gospels about the four men who brought a paralytic to Jesus. When they could not get through the crowd, they opened up the roof of the house and lifted the person up over the wall and down into the building where Jesus was. Building an elevator, creating accessibility, is today's fulfillment of the opening of the house in Jesus' day.

The members of Villa Park Congregational Church, Villa Park, Illinois, recognized that a very simple ramp would make all the educational buildings and offices available, but their primary concern was the attitudinal barrier. The planning was orchestrated by the pastor and several members of the standing committees. They utilized their own resources, including one ordained member (who has since become Conference Minister of the Massachusetts United Church Conference), personnel from the area leadership, and an intentional approach based on the Healing Community certificate to raise the consciousness of the whole congregation.

In Springboro, Ohio, William Gay, pastor of the United Church of Christ, meets with parents of severely handicapped young people in the community. These young people have an urgent need to talk, to share, and to overcome their feelings of being particularly singled out.

First Christian Church in New Castle, Indiana, has a loan program. Walkers and wheelchairs, donated to the church, are loaned to persons with particular need.

Half a dozen Baptist churches in North Carolina (reported in *Biblical Recorder*, January 13, 1979) include: Leeland Church conducting special classes for hearing and non-hearing; Penelope Church in Hickory planning a ramp and the renovation of restrooms; Rockingham First Church reserving parking space for the handicapped; Providence Church in Charlotte starting an elevator fund so that all buildings will be accessible to all members, at a cost of twenty-five thousand dollars; Rick Fork Church near Thomasville sending wheelchairs to the Baptist Hospital in Brazil; Guess Road Church in Durham installing an elevator "so there is not even one step to climb"; Matthews

Church starting a special fund to provide ramps and other changes.

Over and over churches are recognizing that people with heart difficulties, new hips, or the otherwise disabled cannot get to the worship services. In some cases when the pastor mentioned the need immediately the response was, "Let's do it!"

Members of Friedens United Church of Christ in Bern, Kansas, decided not to single out the handicapped by installing an elevator or chairlift. Instead they renovated the entire building, putting on an addition to the church, making a new entrance, turning the sanctuary around, making it totally accessible. They came to this decision because the church realized "a whole family includes the handicapped and elderly sharing together in worship, fellowship, and service projects to others."[2]

One church in St. Louis, in a brainstorming session, drew up the following laundry list:

1. Elevators
2. Good sound systems
3. Reserved parking spaces
4. Church school classes for retarded persons
5. Outdoor parking lot services for handicapped people from May to September
6. A telephone chain for shut-ins
7. A Scout Troop for retarded persons
8. Large-print hymnals for partially sighted
9. Taped services to shut-ins ("The Reel" church)
10. Wheelchairs at the church
11. A handicapped person on the Board of Trustees
12. An interpreter to "speak" to the deaf in a side chapel

13. A task force to explore liturgical needs and possibilities for the developmentally disabled and to establish a residential group home for retarded adults
14. Vacation church school emphasis on Jesus' ministry with the disabled
15. Radio broadcasts
16. Closed circuit television for those unable to climb the steps
17. Toilet facilities for persons with handicaps

Done, yet not done. There is always more. Perhaps the best benediction for this chaper is the word of Muhammad Ali, explaining his recent creation of a program in the Bronx for elderly handicapped: "I have a soft spot for old people, especially the handicapped. Service to others is the rent I pay for my room here on earth."

RESOURCES

This final section of the book provides an easy access to those materials of most importance for the church, synagogue, or other religious agencies in responding to concerns for and with individuals with handicaps.

The first place to go in beginning a program in the local church is the national denominational office, or the office in the area, association, presbytery, synod, conference, or diocese. For example, the Roman Catholic Church has a committee on the handicapped in every local diocese.

At the same time, use the lists suggested here. Remember that printing, postage, and handling cost money, so be prepared to pay for materials.

Since resources change radically over the course of several years, the list is simplified. We assume the most recent materials can be secured from denominational or diocesan headquarters or from other sources whose addresses are given.

So many articles and pamphlets in this area are now being published that a list is outdated within a year. Write to your denominational headquarters or to the other places listed.

The local congregation's point of view is primary in all these listings. Other lists are available for the theological education and for specific areas of work and expertise.

BOOKS

BIBLIOGRAPHICAL

Carlson, Earl R., M.D. *Born That Way.* New York: The John Day Co., 1941.
A classic, this medically oriented book relates Dr. Carlson's own response to cerebral palsy.

Miers, Earl S. *The Trouble Bush.* Chicago: Rand McNally & Co., 1966.
Most felicitous in language, incredibly so, and solid in concept, this classic is an autobiography by a historian and English teacher who wrote and published fifty other books. One of the best!

Spencer, Peter. *No Man an Island.* With Eileen Waugh. London: Triton Books, 1970.
A Royal Air Force pilot, who on his last mission tragically loses his arms, writes lucidly about his road back.

Tulloch, Janet. *Happy Issue: My Handicap and the Church.* With Cynthia Wedel.
Tulloch writes not only about her personal response to her cerebral palsy, but also about the church's response to it and about herself as a person. Personal and warm, she may be charged with being optimistic, but her more recent book on the nursing home situation displays her basic sense of reality.

Wallace, Marjorie, and Robson, Michael. *Suffer the Children.* London: Times Books,
The story of Terry Wiles, one of the most severely handicapped of the "thalidomide babies." I couldn't put it down.

THE MEANING OF DISABILITY

Schoonover, Melvin E. *Letters to Polly . . . On the Gift of Affliction.* Grand Rapids: William B. Eerdmans Publishing Co., 1971.

A teacher in New York Theological Seminary who uses a wheelchair wrote to his daughter, afflicted with osteogenesis imperfecta, about the meaning of her life. One of the best on how to live with hope, joy, bitterness, frustration, and all the burdens of affliction. The letters are filled with the joy and confidence that the author found in Jesus of Nazareth (in which "the walls of separation between human beings shall be torn down").

Steensma, Juliana. *The Quality of Mercy*. Richmond: John Knox Press, 1969.

The story of John Steensma at work in Korea. Most helpful.

Wilke, Harold H. *Strengthened with Might*. Philadelphia: The Westminster Press, 1952.

Some very good quotes. Out of print but may be found in libraries.

INSTITUTIONAL AND SOCIETAL RESPONSES TO HANDICAPPING

Goldenson, Robert M. *Disability and Rehabilitation Handbook*. New York: McGraw-Hill Book Co., 1978.

A new major work.

Viscardi, Henry, Jr. *The Abilities Story*. Middlebury, Vt.: Paul S. Eriksson, Publisher, 1971.

Implementing the right to work for handicapped persons, in a dramatic mixture of institutional and extra-institutional sharing. Himself a tremendous and vital person, "Hank" Viscardi runs a shop and meets bills.

A THEOLOGICAL LOOK AT HANDCAPPING

Soelle, Dorotha. *Suffering*. Trans. by Everett R. Kalin. Philadelphia: Fortress Press, 1975.

A distinguished professor at Union Seminary states that "only those who themselves are suffering will work for the abolition of conditions under which people are exposed to unnecessary suffering." A look at the causes and meaning of suffering.

SEXUALITY AND THE HANDICAPPED

Heslinga, K. *Not Made of Stone: The Sexual Problems of Handicapped People*. Springfield, Ill.: Charles C. Thomas, Publisher, 1974.

A professionally directed book, with a great deal of data, many helps suggested, and a basically open attitude expressed.

Nordqvist, Inger. *Life Together—The Situation of the Handicapped.* Sweden: Fack.

A tightly compressed and beautiful book on various aspects of sexuality and the handicapped.

THE HELPING PROFESSIONS, FINDING RESOURCES

Ayrault, Evelyn W *Helping the Handicapped Teenager Mature.* New York: Association Press, 1971.

Assisting parents and therapists, it is also written for the benefit of the young handicapped teen-ager and provides an excellent directory of many services across the country.

Colston, Lowell. *Pastoral Care With Handicapped Persons.* Philadelphia: Fortress Press, 1978.

Lippman, Leopold, and Goldberg, I. Ignacy. *Right to Education: Anatomy of the Pennsylvania Case and Its Implications for Exceptional Children.* Columbia, N.Y.: Teachers College Press, 1973.

Weiner, Florence *Help for the Handicapped Child.* New York: McGraw-Hill Book Co., 1973.

Where to find help for allergies, arthritis, birth defects down to sickle cell anemia and venereal disease.

White, Emma Jane, ed , *Let's Do More with Persons with Disabilities,* Board of Discipleship of The United Methodist Church. Nashville: Ministries *with* the handicapped and others of special need. A sourcebook for the church.

AUDIOVISUALS

Like Other People, 16mm film, 36 min. Deals with sexual, emotional, and social needs of mentally retarded and physically handicapped people. Describes a relationship between a man and a woman who have epilepsy. Rental. color, $37.50. For information contact Perennial Education, Inc., P.O. Box 236, 1825 Willow Road, Northfield, Illinois 60093.

What Can One Church Do? 35mm filmstrip. Includes script and study guide. Slides by Robert Wihnyk; narration by Ralph E. Ahlberg. Sponsored by U.C.C. Advisory Committee on the Church and the Handicapped. Rental: $5.

Who Are the Debolts and Where Did They Get 19 Kids? For information write: Film Feedback, Communication Commission, National Council of Chuches, Box 500, Manhattenville Station, New York, New York 10027.

Handicappism. Slide show, "Handicappism" HPP-7. Deals with prejudice, stereotyping, and discrimination practiced against disabled persons. Available from Human Policy Press, P.O. Box 127, University Station, Syracuse, New York 13210.

Stones in the Stream. Two-part slide show. Deals with stereotyping and suggested ways for the congregation to change its point of view. Available from United Presbyterian Church, U.S.A. Headquarters, Interchurch Center, 475 Riverside Drive, New York, New York 10027.

ORGANIZATIONS

Closer Look
Box 1492, Washington, D.C. 20013
A national information center for the use of parents of handicapped children and for youth. This center gives practical advice on funding educational programs and other special services. Funded by HEW. Publications: *Report from Closer Look* (a newsletter) and *Practical Advice to Parents.*
The President's Committee on the Employment of the Handicapped Washington, D.C. 20210—202-961-5401

American Coalition of Citizens with Disabilities, Inc.,
1346 Connecticut Avenue., N.W., Suite 817
Washington, D.C. 20036
National umbrella association of sixty-five organizations of and for disabled persons. Works for full realization of human and civil rights of disabled person.
Office of Handicapped Individuals
Office for Human Development
U.S. Department of Health, Education, and Welfare
200 Independence Avenue, S.W., Washington, D.C. 20201

Bureau of Education for the Handicapped, U.S. Department of Health, Education and Welfare, Donohue Building, Washington, D.C. 20202
Rehabilitation Services Administration
Office of Human Development
U.S. Department of Health, Education, and Welfare
330 C. Street S.W., Washington, D.C. 20201
Office for Civil Rights
Office of the Secretary
U.S. Department of Health, Education, and Welfare
330 Independence Avenue, S.W., Washington, D.C. 20207

RESOURCES

Council for Exceptional Children
1920 Association Drive, Reston, Virginia 22091
John Milton Society for the Blind
29 West 34th Street, Sixth Floor, New York, New York 10001
National Association for Retarded Citizens
2709 Avenue E East, Arlington, Texas 76011
Principal publication: *Mental Retardation News,* 10 times a year.
National Easter Seal Society
2023 West Ogden Avenue, Chicago, Illinois 60610
The Easter Seal Society has probably the best set of materials for persons in local congregations who work with the handicapped. Write for an order blank.
Regional Rehabilitation Research Institute on Attitudinal, Legal and Leisure Barriers
George Washington University
1828 L Street, N.W., Suite 704
Washington, D.C. 20036.
A series of helpful pamphlets, one copy free. Write for order blank.

RELIGIOUS RESOURCE GROUPS

United States

Your own church headquarters, national or regional.
Healing Community, 139 Walworth Avenue, White Plains, New York 10606.
National Council of Churches, Department of Christian Education, 475 Riverside Drive, New York, New York 10027.
Mainstream of Riverside Church, Riverside Drive at Reinhold Niebuhr Place (unique example of a local church that developed a program for access, both within its own walls and within the institutions and neighborhoods surrounding it).
Ministry with the Handicapped, DLMC/DDMA, The American Lutheran Church, 422 South Fifth Street, Minneapolis, Minnesota 55415. Publication: *Guidelines for Congregations.*
Accessibility in Religion: A task force within the Catholic Church. Director, Vicki Cox Stanton, Apartment 416, 2445-15th Street, N.W. Washington, D.C. 20009.
Handicapped Encounter Christ, Mr. John Keek, Founder, Palen Road, Hopewell Junction, New York 12533.
Citizen Advocacy, Knights of Columbus, 4331 Lindell Boulevard, St. Louis, Missouri 63108.
The Rev. Morman Leach, Healing Community, 944 Market Street, San Francisco, California 94102.

CREATING THE CARING CONGREGATION

The Rev. Norman Leach, Healing Community, 944 Market Street, San Francisco, California 94102.

Division of Parish Service Lutheran Church in America, 2900 Queen Lane, Philadelphia, Pennsylvania 19129.

Outlook Central Florida Inc., P.O. Box 208, Longwood, Florida 32750.

Europe

Healing Community, c/o Foundation for Disabled Living, 39 Hyde Park Gate, London, England SW 75 DS.

Accessibility Concerns for Churches and Religious Communities, Mrs. Anne Henshall, Principal, Selly Oaks Colleges, Birmingham, England.

Dr. Ferdinand Schlingensiepen, Director, Kaiserswerth, 121 Alte Landstrasse, Kaiserswerth, Dusseldorf, West Germany.

The Task Force on Church and Disability, World Council of Churches, c/o Faith and Order, 50 Route De Ferney, Geneva, Switzerland.

NOTES

Chapter Two

1. From the *Jewish Encyclopedia,* p. 1084.

Chapter Three

1. Frank Bowe, *Handicapping America* (New York: Harper & Row, 1978).

Chapter Four

1. *Study Encounter,* Vol. VII, No. 4, 1971.
2. Ruth Elizabeth Knapp in *One World,* June 1977, No. 27.
3. *One World,* June 1977, p. 9.

Chapter Five

1. "If I Were to Build Again" in *The Christian Ministry,* November 1978.

Chapter Five

1. From the newsletter of Christian League for the Handicapped, Walworth, Wisconsin.
2. Reprinted from *The Cotton Patch Version of Paul's Epistles,* by Clarence Jordan. Used by permission.

Chapter Seven

1. Purd E. Deitz, "We Would Be Building."
2. Reported by Gordon Epps in *United Church News of Kansas,* February 1979.